M000011556

For
Faith

&
Family

For

Faith

Changing America by

&

Family

Strengthening the Family

Dr. Richard Land
with John Perry

BROADMAN
&HOLMAN
PUBLISHERS

Nashville, Tennessee

© 2002
by Richard Land
All rights reserved
Printed in the United States of America

0–8054–2380–X
Published by Broadman & Holman Publishers, Nashville, Tennessee

Published in association with Alive Communications, Inc., 7680 Goddard
Street, Suite 200, Colorado Springs, Colorado 80920.

Heading: CHRISTIAN LIVING

Unless otherwise noted, Old Testament Scripture quotations are from
the Holy Bible, New International Version, copyright © 1973, 1978,
1984 by International Bible Society. Unless otherwise noted, New
Testament Scripture quotations are from the Holman Christian Standard
Bible, © 2000 by Holman Bible Publishers. Used by Permission. Other
versions are identified as follows: KJV, King James Version. NKJV, New
King James Version, copyright © 1979, 1980, 1982, Thomas Nelson,
Inc., Publishers. NLT, Holy Bible, New Living Translation, copyright ©
1996. Used by permission of Tyndale House Publishers, Inc., Wheaton,
Illinois 60189. All rights reserved.

3 4 5 6 7 8 9 10 06 05 04 03 02

TO MOM AND DAD
Who first told me that Jesus loved me and
that God had a wonderful plan for my life

CONTENTS

PREFACE

Why another book on faith and family? Hundreds of books have poured forth from Christian publishers in the past few years as Christians have confronted, and experienced, the ever more devastating impact of the ever heart-breaking disintegration of ever-growing numbers of American families.

America is facing the deepest moral and spiritual crisis in her history. And the only sufficient cure for her potentially terminal illness is found in the Christian faith, what that faith has to say about the divinely ordained institution of the family, and what converts to that faith are empowered by God to do in and through their families.

I grew up in a devout Christian home in a working-class neighborhood in 1950s Houston, Texas. I am very grateful for that very traditional upbringing, which taught me many invaluable foundational truths. First, I learned that the Christian faith is not a religion, but a personal relationship between Jesus and each individual who trusts Him as Lord and Savior. Second, I learned that the Bible was God's Holy Word, fully authoritative, without mistake or error, and sufficient "for doctrine, for reproof, for correction, for instruction in righteousness" (2 Tim. 3:16 NKJV).

Unfortunately, growing up in Baptist churches of that era, I also was taught that Baptists believed in a spiritual Gospel that did not deal with social issues, unless they dealt directly with personal behaviors such as sex, drugs, liquor, or tobacco. To get involved in social issues was considered "a violation of separation of church and state." Over the years since, I have learned better. I now understand that Christ's command to be salt and light demands that as his disciples we must go out into society and seek to make a difference for that which is right and good, just as we are commanded to do in our families.

I now have a much better *perspective*. Growing up in Texas with a fifth-generation Texan as a father and a mother from Boston, I received a unique gift: Texas with *perspective*. I was immersed in the great Texas heritage, with the "never give up" tradition of the Alamo and the sheer sense of possibility which permeates the air in Big Sky Country—but with a Bostonian mother whispering in my ear that biggest was not always best and loudest was not always wisest—*perspective*.

Just so, I have learned to understand the tremendous born-again heritage that is the foundation of Christianity, with a vitally important additional *perspective:* the command to be salt and light in society. I believe God called me to share that vital *perspective* with all my Christian brothers and sisters and to call them to live that full-orbed Christianity that can make such a life-changing difference both in their families and in America.

I believe God has sent all of us as believers "to the kingdom for such a time as this" (Esther 4:14 KJV), and that if we give him the obedience that calls down his blessings upon us, He will indeed "repay you for the years the locusts have eaten" (Joel 2:25).

Thanks for listening! God bless you, God bless your family, and God bless America!

Richard Land
Nashville, Tennessee

ACKNOWLEDGMENTS

I am grateful for the contributions of many friends and colleagues who shared in the creation of this project. It was truly a team effort, and I am sincerely grateful to all who served in this task, especially my fellow Oxonian, John Perry, who is the best writing partner an author would desire. His research, reading, gathering of facts, deciphering of my disgraphic scribblings, and following me around with a tape recorder were invaluable. This project would never have happened without John's help.

I am thankful to my parents to whom this book is dedicated. I am also deeply thankful for my wife, Becky, and my three children, Jennifer, Richard Jr., and Rachel, who are so indescribably special to me and have helped shape the content of this book in so many ways. My two proudest titles are husband and dad.

I would also like to express my gratitude to my diligent staff who labor above and beyond the call of duty. God has given me an incredible ministry team for which I am very appreciative. Thank you—Kerry Bural, Pat Clark, Karen Cole, Wayne Cole, Kim Coleman, Tim Cuffman, Barrett Duke, Harold Harper, Dwayne Hastings, Matt Hawkins, Laura Headley, Barbara Jester, Lana Kimbro, Judy Lawson, Ben Mitchell, Steve Nelson, Jerry Price, Bobby Reed, Shannon Royce, King Sanders, Tom Strode, Brian Terrell, June Turner, Sulyn Wilkins, and Dawn Wyatt.

Thanks also to all of my co-laborers and partners in the harvest who listen to our radio program daily, who pray for our ministry, and who support us financially. Your prayers and letters of encouragement mean a great deal to our staff and to me personally.

Most of all, I am grateful for my Heavenly Father and God's Son, my Savior, the coming King, Jesus the Christ. May He use this book for His kingdom and His glory.

INTRODUCTION

The institution of the family has served for all of history as the bedrock of society. The marriage of one man and one woman is the fount out of which flows the critical values that sustain and benefit societies. As Linda J. Waite and Maggie Gallagher write in *The Case for Marriage,* "There is incontrovertible sociological evidence that proves that when marriages fail, families are weakened; and when families are weakened, society as a whole feels the impact." It was not happenstance that the first institution established by God was marriage.

As you read this book it is my prayer that you will have a better understanding that God has ordained three institutions in human society to enable individuals to fulfill their God-given purposes: the family, the church, and civil government. Each of these institutions is indispensable and each makes certain, uniquely valuable contributions to society. If any of these institutions is impaired, society will suffer in very specific ways. If the church is undermined, people will have a reduced opportunity to hear the counsel of God; if civil government is undermined, the people are not protected from predatory evil; and if the institution of marriage is undermined, families suffer, with the weakest and most defenseless among us—the children—suffering the most grievously. If any of these three institutions seeks to dominate the legitimate sphere of another or surrenders its proper sphere of influence, society's very foundations are imperiled.

I felt led to write this book because the family is a critically important institution. It is within the family that children learn the vital attributes of compassion and mercy—essential elements that compel us to care for the weak in society. Family members learn how to cooperate with each other, an essential social trait that enables individuals to combine their energies to accomplish great things for God. They learn the value of making and keeping commitments to others, an indispensable characteristic that assures unity and success in our God-given purposes. Most importantly, in families individuals learn to sacrifice for the needs of others, the linchpin of healthy human relationships and a strong society. A family established upon the marriage between a man and woman provides for the cultivation of these characteristics in ways that other relationships do not. Sadly, many marriages today fail to develop and model these characteristics. By their very nature, broken marriages and counterfeit alternative relationships such as cohabitation and same-sex unions fail to impact, bless, and benefit society in the manifold ways that intact, committed, heterosexual marriages do.

While marriages between men and women are the primary source of society's bedrock values, this critically important institution is under severe assault today. Divorce, same-sex marriages, premarital sex, pornography, substance abuse, negligence in fulfilling family responsibilities, and a myriad of other failings occur too often in marriages. Such failings occur with equal frequency among churchgoers and nonchurchgoers. Consequently, today the very foundation of society is threatened. For without the purest forms of compassion, mercy, cooperation, commitment, and sacrifice flowing out of strong heterosexual marriages, there is little prospect for the endurance and expansion of a just and civil society.

Given this bleak prospect, it is imperative that we redouble our efforts to build strong marriages. If we fail in this responsibility, families, and society itself suffer.

I pray that all who read this book will recognize their divine importance in God's grand design for humanity and recommit themselves to building strong families, strengthening weak ones, and restoring broken ones. On the heels of its primary responsibility to reach the entire world with the Gospel of Jesus Christ, the church's next most critical contribution to society is its responsibility to lay the foundation for the building of strong families. May God equip and empower us by His Holy Spirit to be instruments that encourage rock-solid families built on the foundation of the Solid Rock—the Lord Jesus Christ.

CHAPTER I

HUNKER IN THE BUNKER

YOU CAN'T COUNTER THE CULTURE WHILE YOU'RE COWERING.

For people committed to Christian values, popular American culture at the start of the new millennium often may appear to be a hopeless case. In the name of free speech, artistic expression, tolerance, and self-determination, contemporary culture has grown gradually but relentlessly more coarse, more brutal, and more outrageous to the point where it has all but lost its power to shock.

The music, movies, television shows, and pictures that bombard us every day would have been unimaginable even a decade ago: nudity, extreme violence, profanity, perversity of every imaginable type (and some frankly unimaginable), all in the name of entertainment, freedom, and profitability. As the public grows more jaded, the words and images grow ever more graphic, gritty, and gruesome in order to "keep the customer satisfied."

At the same time, our culture has been threatened like never before by the increase in and "normalization" of premarital and extramarital sexual relations, divorce, sexually transmitted diseases, single-parent households, child abuse, and a host of other problems that are shaking the foundations of the American family. Leaders and policymakers have wisely recognized the dangers of some behaviors and have taken important and responsible steps toward eliminating or at least discouraging them. But when it comes to preserving the family, many of today's lawmakers and public figures are often neutral at best. At worst, they're an active threat to the very Judeo-Christian traditions upon which our democratic laws are based and without which they will ultimately fail.

WHAT'S THE GOVERNMENT'S GENERAL POSITION ON TRADITIONAL CHRISTIAN VALUES?

The process our community leaders use to decide which life-threatening trends they will challenge and which they will ignore (or even endorse) is a real puzzle to me. Scientists tell us that smoking is dangerous. Its hazards are indisputably documented by wave after wave of scientific evidence. People who smoke regularly have a far higher risk of death by cancer than people who don't. And so there's a nationwide ban on radio and TV advertising of tobacco products, laws have curtailed public smoking everywhere from restaurants to football stadiums, and millions of dollars in public funds are spent encouraging people not to smoke.

At the same time, scientists tell us that exposure to AIDS is far more deadly than exposure to tobacco: there's virtually a 100-percent chance that if you get AIDS it will eventually kill you. Yet for all the public service campaigns funded with your and my tax dollars warning Americans not to smoke, there is little or nothing spent warning them not to have sex outside of marriage. Such a campaign might well reduce new cases of AIDS overnight and save countless thousands of lives. Smoking is bad, the government says, but nonmarital sex is a "lifestyle choice."

So where are we? The media bombards us with sex and violence, the traditional family is fractured by sex and violence as a direct result, and the government that should protect us has turned the chicken coop over to the foxes, ironically abandoning the Judeo-Christian traditional values our freedoms were built upon—in the name of freedom. The First Amendment has been turned on its head.

If I weren't a Christian, I'd be worried. Honestly, deep down inside, I do fear for the future of our country and our cherished freedoms and way of life, which is without a doubt the richest and freest in the history of the world.

WHAT'S THE CHRISTIAN RESPONSE TO THIS "NEW MORALITY"?

Many well-meaning and faithful Christians are worried about our future, and they have a right to be. Fifty years ago popular American culture reflected Judeo-Christian values. Today the situation has turned 180 degrees, and American public policy specifically and categorically too often shuts out those values. While the First Amendment right to free speech is zealously—and often successfully—claimed by pornographers to legitimize their trade, too often Christian students are denied the freedom to pray together in schools or hold voluntary Bible studies at free times during the school day. By some measure, it seems, pornographic free speech is now more legal than the Christian variety.

It's a helpless feeling. Our fallen culture spills over on us from every direction like waste from a leaky sewer pipe. What do we do about it?

All too often, the Christian response is to stand there with our mouths half open for a minute or two, then hunker in the bunker: withdraw from the rawness and coarseness and evil in the world and stay home; throw out the TV; unhook ourselves from a threatening world. Families find themselves trapped in survival mode.

While such a strategy is understandable, there are two things wrong with it. First, it won't work. Unless you live on a deserted island, you and your family are part of the culture of our time, like it or not. Second, it's contrary to God's plan. In spite of the challenges and difficulties, the Bible calls Christians to be salt and light in the world.

But, you ask, *what if you're burned out by trying to hold on to your values when everybody else has abandoned theirs? How can you be salt and light if you're toast?*

It's ironic that the times in our lives when the lessons in the Bible can do us the most good are the times when we most tend to forget about them. The fact is that the Bible sitting on your bookshelf or beside your bed or on your desk or in the back of a drawer somewhere gives you everything you need to know to counter the culture and send immoral forces running for cover instead of the other way around.

What can I do to restore traditional morals?

Here's the good news: Christian families are never helpless against the tide of godless and dangerous influences in our culture as long as they read and heed the inerrant Word of God. Do that, and you have nothing to fear. Others who have worked diligently and taken the Scriptures to heart have achieved some remarkable and encouraging successes that I will share with you a little later. But you have to have faith. You have to climb out of your bunker. You'll never win a battle, much less the war, hiding from the enemy.

This is easy to say and hard to do. There are literally hundreds of Bible verses encouraging Christians to stand fast in their faith in a fallen world. But in the heat of battle—talking with your family, writing your city councilman—defending the faith in whatever arenas God places before you can be very hard and the constant pressure can simply wear you down.

Are you living your life believing Christ will support you in your struggles and lead you to ultimate victory over the cultural forces that stand in opposition to a Christian worldview? Or are you just hoping to make it through another day?

WHAT MAKES THE FAMILY SO CRUCIAL FOR MAINTAINING MORAL STANDARDS?

The family is one of only three divinely ordained institutions in all of creation (the others are the church and the civil authorities). The family relationship is something everybody on earth has in common: we were all born into a family. It's where the assurance of Christ's love and power should begin. True national security is not going to be found in weapons; it's not going to be found in our armed might, though that's important. If there's no one with passion and commitment to man the barricades, the barricades can't help us. True security is going to be found in the moral fiber and structure of our families, and in whether or not we are godly people.

The family is the essential center of culture and society; it's where culture and society have their origins. If we're going to be godly people, we've got to have godly homes. The key ingredients to a godly home are a godly mom and dad who are loving and praying for their children and who acknowledge that God is the head of their home. The core of a solid family is a marriage founded in the rock that is Jesus Christ.

Few things are a more effective witness, a more effective way to be salt and light to both your children and community, than to have the marriage God wants you to have and for you to be the husband or wife God wants you to be. But as we've seen, the traditional family is under fire like never before in American history. There's little point in debating for long the problems and challenges American families face because they're well documented already. But we do have to examine and understand them before we move on to an infinitely more important question: what can a family—your family—do to stand confidently and successfully against declining moral and cultural standards?

How can you not only stand fast, but move against the trend?

WHAT DO OUR GENERATION'S DEEP THINKERS THINK ABOUT BIBLE-BASED MORALITY?

Every Christian family in America can take a stand for what's right and godly, and for the traditional values that made our nation the freest, strongest, and most prosperous nation in the history of the world.

The secularization and coarsening of our culture has been under way for many years. Various writers, preachers, and commentators have pointed out the increasing dominance of an antispiritual, naturalistic, and secular bias throughout the last half of the twentieth century, the bloodiest century in the history of mankind. As early as 1946, Carl F. H. Henry called attention to the secular philosophy of humanism, which states that the ultimate source of truth and right is within humanity, and naturalism, which says ultimate truth is found in science and nature.

In 1949 T. S. Eliot, the famous American-born British poet, playwright, and Nobel Laureate, warned of the decision Western civilization faced, describing it as "an inevitable choice between a reassertion of Judeo-Christian values in Western culture or an acquiescence to an emerging pagan, humanistic culture."

In his commencement address at Harvard University in June of 1978, another Nobel Prize winner, the heroic Soviet dissident Alexandr Solzhenitsyn, warned of the grievous consequences of worshiping things on earth to the detriment of things above: "The humanistic way of thinking which has proclaimed itself our guide did not admit the existence of intrinsic evil in man. Nor did it see any task higher than the attainment of happiness on earth."

This thought pattern, he concluded, "started Western civilization on the dangerous trend of worshiping Man and his material needs as if human life had no higher meaning." In other words, we must restore traditional Judeo-Christian values to our culture, or else continue on a dangerous, downward path toward moral emptiness and spiritual darkness.

CAN WE LEGISLATE MORALITY? SHOULD WE?

This brings us face-to-face with the politician's and protester's oft-heard cry, "You can't legislate morality." Of course you can. And of course we must.

The fact is that every law we have is based on moral principles. Laws against murder, theft, rape, and racism are the legislation of morality. As a society we think it's morally wrong to settle an argument by killing someone. Some societies— natives in the Amazon jungle of Ecuador, for example—consider it perfectly legitimate to resolve a disagreement by killing the other party. Yet when we pass laws making murder and theft and rape and racism illegal, we are not so much trying to impose our morality on murderers and thieves and rapists and racists as we are trying to keep them from imposing their immorality on their unwilling victims.

Every law carries the weight of cultural morality. Otherwise there would be no justification for a law that punishes me for stealing something of yours because I want it. And it is our right and our obligation as Christian believers to ensure that the morality of our laws reflects the Judeo-Christian values of Jesus and the Old and New Testaments because biblical morality has been, and must continue to be, the foundation for culture.

We also have to stand fast when pollsters and bureaucrats assure us, in slightly condescending and self-righteous tones, that there really isn't a problem. By every measure, the family in America is growing steadily more dysfunctional as it reels under the impact of societal blows and pagan parental behavior. The nuclear family as we have known it in the Judeo-Christian West is so shattered that concerted efforts are now being made to redefine it to fit the new prevailing reality. If traditional families are so at odds with current trends, then the popular solution too often is to change the public's idea of what a successful family should be.

WHAT'S THE TWENTY-FIRST CENTURY DEFINITION OF A FAMILY?

The traditional definition for a family now and always, at least as God intended it, is a husband and wife sharing their lives in marriage and their children. Of course there are extended families that include grandparents or an orphaned cousin or an aunt who never married, but these are almost always formed around the father/mother core. Today, many contemporary family "experts" claim that a "family" should be considered almost any combination of people living under one roof: unmarried couples with or without children, homosexual couples, communal groups, and so on.

Well-meaning social workers and counselors often attempt to solve the far-reaching problem of family fragmentation by claiming there is nothing wrong. They want to describe what *is* as normal instead of what God intended as normal. This is a recipe for disaster. There's a vital difference between understanding the problems that arise when there is no father or no mother in the house and saying children don't need a father or a mother.

From prime-time television to public assistance workers the message is pounded into us that parents, especially fathers, are optional. This is a fatal assumption on the part of many of our policy makers today, and if we as Christians don't point that out to society, who will? If we won't stand in the gap and provide family relationships for those without them, who will?

How can I make God's family standard America's standard again?

Timidness and lack of resolve have led us to chafe under non-Christian or anti-Christian public policies. The bigger issue though is what God must think about the way things are going. When you and I stand before Him and give an account of ourselves, will He ask us why were we not about our Father's business? Often it's not that we don't see the need or don't want to do something; we just don't know where or how to start.

The family has all but ceased to function in a nurturing, moralizing way in major segments of American culture. And I'm not just talking about the ghettoes of our inner cities, as forlorn, tragic, and hopeless as those dwelling places of the semipermanent underclass often appear to be. There's a moral imperative for change. For the self-proclaimed nonreligious, there's an appeal to their enlightened self-interest. You don't have to be a Jew or Christian to see the life-changing advantage of traditional Judeo-Christian, American moral values.

I doubt we can survive as the nation we've known if we allow a permanent underclass of underprivileged young people to waste away in our cities. They have a life experience and a value system that is as alien from many of ours as if they had been raised on the dark side of the moon. Having realized how far the family has fallen from God's divinely ordained institution—a husband and father, a wife and mother, and children—we must reawaken in our own hearts and the hearts of others a clear understanding of God's design.

What does real family leadership look like?

The apostle Paul told the Ephesians that husbands are to love their wives (Eph. 5:25). That was a radical, controversial statement in the Ephesians' day and it's still profoundly misunderstood by people who don't know the context. Husbands are to love their wives as Christ loves the church, with the revolutionary, self-sacrificing, other-directed *agape* love with which God first loved us, and which is produced by the Holy Spirit in the hearts of yielded believers. This is not the mere romantic infatuation and physical attraction of late-night cable television. A husband who loves his wife as Christ loved the church will always put his wife's needs ahead of his own.

Leadership according to the Gospel of Jesus Christ is servant leadership. It's sacrificial, foot-washing leadership that gives itself in service to others. This *agape* love was a concept

baptized and consecrated within the church. People character-
ized by *agape* show love without expecting it to be returned,
lend where there is little hope of repayment, give without
reserve or limit, and accept the enmity of the world willingly,
unresistingly, and sacrificially. This is the love of Christ. This
is the love a husband should have for his wife according to the
apostle Paul.

This is the love that will revolutionize relationships inside
and outside the family and enable parents to obey the command not to provoke their children to wrath, but instead to
"bring them up in the training and instruction of the Lord"
(Eph. 6:4b). This love is the means for launching a successful
movement to reclaim the high moral ground in our nation. We
must not only reawaken, we must reconstruct within our
churches and communities of believers a truly biblical understanding of the family as God meant it to be. And we must act
on our beliefs.

ARE THERE ALTERNATIVES TO A BIBLE-BASED FAMILY?

Nothing can replace the family as a nurturing environment for
healthy human growth and emotional and spiritual development. Given that, we have to reassert the Christian family's
unique value and place in society. Then, having reconstructed,
reinstituted, and reasserted the Christian family, we must
reach out and seek to replace the family and be family for
those who either don't have one or who belong to one that is
dysfunctional. Through the power of Jesus Christ we must
allow Him to use us as instruments of healing in families and
to individual family members. As couples, as families, as
churches, we must allow our Heavenly Father to use us as the
fathers, the mothers, the sons, the daughters, the brothers, and

the sisters that bruised spirits and wounded souls need and miss so desperately.

It has never been enough just to say these things. We have to live them. We must live the *agape* love of self-sacrifice that Christians are called to live. As Francis of Assisi put it, "Preach the Gospel all the time. If necessary, use words." How are we to do that? Francis raised the question, and one of his prayers gives us an answer:

> Lord, make me an instrument of Thy peace. Where there is hatred, let me sow love. Where there is injury, pardon. Where there is doubt, faith. Where there is darkness, light. Where there is sadness, joy. Grant that I may not seek to be consoled as to console, to be understood as to understand, to be loved as to love. For it is in giving that we receive, it is in pardoning that we are pardoned, it is in dying that we gain eternal life.

WHAT WOULD AN IDEAL AMERICA LOOK LIKE?

Once at a press conference a reporter asked me this question: "We've heard a lot from you about what's wrong with America. What would America look like if America was the way you wanted it to be?"

I answered, "Well, a good place to start would be America in 1955 without the racism and without the sexual discrimination against women." I said that because America in 1955 was a place where the following things did not happen:

- Less than half of our children currently grow up in intact families. In 1960, 80 percent of our children were reared in homes where the father and mother were both in the home and were married to each other.

- More than a million children a year experience the pain of parental divorce.
- There has been in the last ten years a 400-percent increase in child abuse significant enough to require a doctor's attention.
- Every hour our children watch 78 violent acts on television.
- Every day in America 2,795 teenage girls get pregnant.
- Every day in America 1,106 of those girls snuff out the lives of their unborn children through abortion.
- Every 78 seconds a teenager in America attempts suicide. In the last 30 years the suicide rate of teenage boys has quadrupled; the rate for girls has doubled.
- By the time they graduate from high school, 66 percent of American teenagers acknowledge they have used one or more illegal drugs.

WHAT'S THE GREATEST ENEMY OF TRUTH? HOW CAN I FIGHT IT?

Any way you slice it, absolute standards of propriety and behavior have all but disappeared. We are awash in an ocean of relativism. And yet when Christian believers try to stand up and speak for the truth, we're told, "Oh you can't do that! That's a violation of separation of church and state!"

Such assertions are foolish and dangerous nonsense. John F. Kennedy once said, "The greatest enemy of truth is often not the lie, deliberate, contrived and dishonest, but the myth, persistent, persuasive and unrealistic." And it is a persistent, persuasive and unrealistic myth to say that laws shouldn't reflect faith-based morality. All law is the legislation of somebody's morality. If it isn't God's, then may God help us!

How do we keep a biblical and spiritual perspective in the midst of the churning cauldron of ever-changing opinions and trendy ideas which masquerade as "values" in today's world? How do we impart God's never-changing values in an ever-changing world?

Fortunately, God has given parents a blueprint for how to create a spiritually nurturing atmosphere and at the same time inoculate themselves and their children against the malignant and harmful influences so prevalent in our increasingly sinful world. And it's all centered on the family, not the government, employers, welfare workers or anything else.

In the Book of Deuteronomy, God instructs Moses to tell His people how important it is to remember and obey His commandments as they leave the wilderness and enter the land of plenty. God knew the temptations and pitfalls of prosperity were in some ways even worse than the rigors and privations of the desert wilderness when He gave them "a land with large, flourishing cities you did not build, houses filled with all kinds of good things you did not provide, wells you did not dig, and vineyards and olive groves you did not plant—then when you eat and are satisfied, be careful that you do not forget the LORD, who brought you out of Egypt" (Deut. 6:10–12).

Does that scenario sound familiar? In the twenty-first century, America enjoys a level of prosperity unprecedented in world history. So how are we to remember God's changeless truths? God tells us to love Him with all our heart, soul, and strength and to keep His commandments in our hearts (Deut. 6:5–6). However, for our children to remember Him and His commandments they must first know of Him and His commandments.

God commands parents in particular and adults in general to impress His commandments on children: "Talk about them when you sit at home and when you walk along the road, when you lie down and when you get up. Tie them as symbols on your hands and bind them on your foreheads. Write them on the doorframes of your houses and on your gates" (Deut. 6:7–9).

The New Testament corollary is Ephesians 6:4: "Fathers, don't stir up anger in your children, but bring them up in the training and instruction of the Lord." The original Greek text here implies a steady course of nourishing, which inevitably involves discipline. In another letter, the apostle Paul writes, "As you know, like a father with his own children, we encouraged, comforted, and implored each one of you to walk worthy of God" (1 Thess. 2:11–12). The sixteenth-century reformer Martin Luther had a typically straightforward way of expressing a similar thought: "Spare the rod and spoil the child—that is true: but beside the rod keep an apple to give him when he has done well."

Our world is unimaginably different from the world of Martin Luther or Paul. Though times and cultures change, the basic needs of our humanity do not; our children desperately need the spiritual and moral advice and guidance God expects parents to provide. Even seemingly disdainful teens desperately seek parental involvement and advice. William Damon of the Stanford University Center for Adolescence reminds us that parents need to "share what they really believe in, what they really think is important. These basic values are more important than math skills or SATs." Amazing, isn't it, that his conclusions are so similar to the priorities in Deuteronomy over three thousand years ago! However much the world has changed, the human nature God gave us hasn't changed at all.

HOW SHOULD I PREPARE MY KIDS
FOR THE "REAL WORLD"?

Next to our responsibility to God and to our spouse, raising children is the most important responsibility we have. We must teach them and work conscientiously and diligently to shield them from truly damaging influences such as sexually suggestive and violent entertainment. Powerful and convincing evidence continues to mount that exposure to such material, while not healthy for people of any age, is particularly damaging emotionally to children and adolescents with still-developing minds and personalities.

I frequently hear that children shouldn't be confined in a spiritual hothouse while the gale of secular relativism rages out in the real world. The argument is that it leaves them too soft and unprepared to deal with the harsh challenges of everyday living. I don't buy that for an instant, and I hope you don't buy it either. It is our job as Christian parents to protect young, delicate, uncertain children from being bombarded by relativism and secularism. Then when they're older, they will have been nurtured and strengthened to the point where they can prevail against the destructive influences of secular culture. They can survive the secular storm they will inevitably encounter with their spiritual and moral foundation firmly in place.

There's no greater gift parents can give their children than to rear them in a spiritually nurturing home environment. Children raised that way will indeed rise up and call their parents blessed.

In the prophet Jeremiah's time the only real earthly protection a city had was its wall. There was a watchman there waiting to sound the warning when the city was threatened. God said His prophets were His watchmen.

We must protect our children, and we must be ever watchful and diligent. Who is on the wall right now? In the past forty years the pornography industry has grown more than a hundredfold. In America today there are more hard-core pornography outlets than there are McDonald's. And we wonder why America aborts four thousand babies a day, and why rates of child molestation and rape continue to increase.

I'M READY TO MAKE A DIFFERENCE. WHAT'S MY NEXT STEP?

If America dies, she will die of self-inflicted wounds. This has been the case with great nations throughout history. It happened to the Roman Empire: destruction from without came only after corrosion from within. In the modern era it happened to Great Britain, a worldwide empire for centuries that stood alone against Hitler, but which today has lost its spiritual engine and, as a result, much of its wealth and influence in world affairs as well.

Every law reflects a moral mandate to influence behavior in some direction. Lincoln knew this when he spoke on the slavery issue during the 1860 presidential campaign. I can picture him with his lanky frame and craggy face standing before an audience and declaring, "You say you will not let me do a single thing to say slavery is wrong. There's no place where you will even allow me to call it wrong. We must not call it wrong in the slave states because it is there. We must not call it wrong in politics because that's bringing morality into politics, and we must not call it wrong in the pulpit because that's bringing politics into religion." Lincoln correctly framed this alleged dilemma. All legislation makes a moral statement. If you can't legislate morality, you can't legislate anything, ever.

Unfortunately, Christians have allowed themselves to believe the lie that somehow they don't have a right and an obligation to be involved in public policy. They've withdrawn and left the field to the enemy. Jesus said to us, "You are the salt of the earth. . . . You are the light of the world" (Matt. 5:13–14). Salt is a preservative and a purifying agent, but it must come in contact with what it's preserving. It must touch what it will purify. In doing so, it also stings and irritates. Sometimes, as salt and light, we are called to sting and irritate.

In bringing about changes, we can't look for the government to save us. When King Josiah died, his reforms died with him. We have to be involved in the political process—we have to be the government if we ever expect the government to embrace our worldview. Through the legislative process and the ballot box, Christians must send the unequivocal message to the government to quit suppressing our right to be involved. We want the government to guarantee a level playing field, then get off the field!

But before we can take our faith to the public forum, we have to have it right in our own hearts and in our families. As God promised us in 2 Chronicles 7:14, "If my people, who are called by my name, will humble themselves and pray and seek my face and turn from their wicked ways, then will I hear from heaven and will forgive their sin and will heal their land." Sounds like a pretty fair trade to me. So where do we go from here?

CHAPTER 2

SALT AND LIGHT

Discussions about moral issues these days tend to degenerate into arguments over whose morality we're talking about. The popular view is that morality is on some sort of dimmer switch we can turn up and down to suit the needs and agendas of the moment. As we've seen, that has produced a world of relativism, where there are no absolutes of right and wrong.

The Bible tells us that there *are* absolutes of right and wrong. It doesn't say we have to like it or agree with it, but there's absolutely no doubt they exist. Pollster George Gallup, who has a worldwide reputation for accuracy in researching and interpreting specific, precise facts about our culture, reports that our greatest problems are not bread-and-butter issues, but issues of faith.

Gallup writes, "I would venture to say that the great problems of our time are not economic and political, but they are religious and moral . . . We are in a moral crisis of the first dimension." If all moral standards are equally good, we couldn't have a moral crisis. The fact that Gallup recognizes a crisis is further proof that we have deviated from a historic norm.

Further proof of how important the discussion of religious morality has become is the comment in a *Wall Street Journal* column during the summer of 2001 that "religious practice is increasingly the main dividing line in American politics." The article quotes Senator Joe Lieberman, a Democrat and Orthodox Jew, who warned his fellow Democrats that they "must earn back the people's trust on matters of value and culture and faith."

Noting that people who attended worship regularly (at least four times a month) voted Republican in the 2000 presidential election by 57 percent to 40 percent, he told the Democratic Leadership Council, "We have too often dismissed and disparaged the importance of faith in American life and made the faithful feel unwelcome in our party, particularly if they are open and outspoken about their religion."

WHAT REALLY CONTROLS AMERICAN CULTURE?

The Bible reminds us that the ultimate stabilizing influence on our culture is the family. Nurturing, spiritual growth, concern for others, compassion, and other essential components of a safe, healthy, strong, vital culture—of which the United States is the most successful example in the history of the world—all begin with the family. The surest way to change the culture is through the family. Political parties, television networks, the Internet, public policy groups, labor unions, and every other instrument of change in our society today are guided by principles first acquired as family members. In the vast majority of cases, the moral attitude of their families became their own moral attitudes.

This relationship between family members and the institutions they control shows how important it is for families to know and follow the teaching of the Bible when it comes to morality. If we want these institutions to promote a biblical worldview, we have to do everything we can to make sure their leaders have strong biblical teaching in their families.

How can I get contemporary culture back on the traditional track?

The first and most essential step to reasserting traditional morality in this country—which was historically an overt Judeo-Christian morality—is to make sure your family follows biblical guidelines for moral thought and behavior. Read the Bible. Pray for understanding. Get involved in a study of the Scriptures. God's Word has the simplest and most certain answers to the complex, heartbreaking moral and spiritual dilemmas we see all around us. And God's answers always work.

The second step to moral renewal in our nation is for you as a member of a Christian family to become involved in community affairs, and to vote your values instead of your political affiliation. Don't get stuck on a politician's label, like Democrat or Republican, Socialist or Independent, and look for candidates who promote decency, accountability, and responsibility framed within biblical standards.

For me, this wisdom has been a long time in coming. I grew up in a bicultural home: my dad's from Texas, and my mother's from Boston. Dad was what they call in Texas a "Yellow Dog" Democrat. He'd vote for the Democrat in any election even if it was a yellow dog. Mother was a "Rock-ribbed" Republican, which is the New England version of the Yellow Dog Democrat.

What I know now is that they were both wrong in 1956, the first national election I remember, when Dad voted for Stevenson and Mother voted for Eisenhower; they were wrong in 1960 when Dad went for Kennedy and Mother supported Nixon; they were wrong about Johnson and Goldwater in 1964 too.

They were wrong because they were voting the traditional party loyalties of their families and regional origins instead of their shared common core values, beliefs, and convictions. Ultimately, our loyalty belongs not to any political party or candidate but to God Almighty. And when the time comes, I believe God will ask you about how you voted and why.

We've been lured into a false belief that true freedom means no rules and no responsibility, that every person, no matter how perverted, is absolutely free to "do his own thing." But freedom without rules isn't democracy; it's anarchy. Benjamin Hooks, former executive director of the NAACP, warned of the shift in America's collective thinking and the dangers it carried when he said, "The whole philosophy of our country has changed . . . [to accept] immorality, degeneracy, pornographic movies. . . . I'm the world's greatest advocate of the First Amendment . . . but somehow we've got to have freedom with some responsibility."

CHRISTIANS ARE SOUNDING THE ALARM ABOUT THE MORAL CRISIS IN AMERICA, AREN'T THEY?

Agnostics and atheists also admit our culture is in crisis, even as they defend the practices that contribute to the crisis: they shake their heads in disgust at fatal school shootings but fight any attempts to block the spread of video games and movies that trivialize and glorify murder; they stare in shock at the rise in sexual crimes but insist that nude dance clubs and Internet porn are constitutional "rights."

Everyone from Martin Luther King Jr. to Chuck Colson has affirmed the desperate need to hold on to a shared view of morality, a morality of absolutes. During the civil rights struggles of the 1960s, King longed for the time when Americans would be judged "not by the color of their skin, but by the content of their character." He knew, and his listeners knew, that the content he was talking about was not to a relative standard, but to a recognized, absolute standard. Otherwise the statement would have been meaningless.

A generation later, Chuck Colson observed in *Christianity Today* that, "Christians must contend for biblically informed morality and justice in the halls of power . . . what we do must flow from what we are."

WHAT'S THE RELATIONSHIP BETWEEN LAW AND MORALITY? WHAT CAN I DO TO IMPROVE IT?

Character judgment defines our legal system today. If we didn't think it was morally wrong to steal, we wouldn't put people in prison for stealing. Every law on the books carries a moral judgment with it. This is consistent with the words of Proverbs 29:18 that say, "Where there is no vision, the people perish" (KJV). Christians and Christian families must proclaim God's changeless standard of truth, holding up the plumb line of God's moral standard to inform, exhort, and convict the people of their desperate need for repentance, regeneration, and revival.

This means that, once you have a sense of what the Bible directs you to do, you need to do it in a visible, confident way. To have the impact God wants you to have, your light must shine before men. Once you know the way God wants you to go, you are ready to exercise your responsibilities as a Christian and your rights as a citizen.

Your involvement is our only hope for curbing the crippling epidemics of alcohol and drug abuse, mindless violence, and rampant materialism that have so debased our society and assailed it with virtually ubiquitous sexual immorality and a pornography-fed vortex of violent sexual crimes against women and children both inside and outside the home.

That is the world of relativism, a world with no absolutes of right and wrong—a world built on the false and tragic notion that human beings can find self-fulfillment apart from God.

WHAT'S THE PROBLEM WITH LETTING EVERYBODY DO THEIR OWN THING ACCORDING TO THEIR OWN CONSCIENCE?

In his wonderful book *The Enduring Revolution,* Chuck Colson eloquently and accurately writes that the myth of relative moral values

> hides the dividing line between good and evil, noble and base. It has thus created a crisis in the realm of truth. When a society abandons its transcendent values, each individual's moral vision becomes purely personal and finally equal. Society becomes merely the sum total of individual preferences, and since no preference is morally preferable, anything that can be dared will be permitted.
>
> This leaves the moral consensus for our laws and manners in tatters. Moral neutrality slips into moral relativism. Tolerance substitutes for truth, indifference for religious conviction.

Relative morality is no morality. And a country governed without moral absolutes cannot last. Look at what today's moral disconnect has done to America's families: 40 percent of ninth graders and 72 percent of twelfth graders are sexually active. Births to unwed mothers have tripled in thirty years.

And time and time again, one of the main reasons cited for America's ills is the decline and fall of the traditional family structure. Fifty percent of schoolchildren come from single-parent or step-parent families; they are 70 percent more likely to be expelled and up to 75 percent more likely to repeat a grade. One of the most reliable predictors of college entrance test scores is whether or not the child's biological father lives in the house.

Set adrift in a relativistic, value-neutral world, surrounded by divorce, decay, neglect, and abuse, our children are in mortal peril. They desperately need us to practice our faith and defend our right to do so, and to raise them "in the training and instruction of the Lord" (Eph. 6:4).

ISN'T IT JUST COMMON SENSE TO REDEFINE THE FAMILY IN TERMS OF TODAY'S LIFESTYLES?

I've got my opinion of what a family is and you've got yours, and the welfare department has its own, but in reality God defines the family and nobody else does. There's nothing common about it. In Genesis 2:18–24, God gives man a helpmate because He knows "it is not good" for man to live alone. The two become one flesh in the sight of God and set the biblical template for families from then on: one man and one woman joined together in the sight of God. This definition is under attack; instead of restoring the family, it's a lot easier to redefine it. The dysfunctional status quo is defined as normal. Husbands are optional and fathers are unnecessary. Married couples with children comprise only 26 percent of American households, a drastic decline from even twenty years ago.

God's Word about the family does not change. We sympathize with single and divorced people, but that doesn't mean we accept them as ideal models for the family. No matter what happens societally, God's model remains one man with one woman for life—not a model we're imposing, but one God has designed for the well-being of the human community. We're not playing God; just passing along His instructions.

TV GETS BLAMED FOR ALL SORTS OF PROBLEMS,
BUT DOESN'T IT SIMPLY REFLECT THE CULTURE
AS IT ALREADY EXISTS?

Søren Kierkegaard, the nineteenth-century Danish philosopher, died more than twenty years before the telephone was invented. Even so, he anticipated what might happen to the shared moral value of a people when farfetched or dangerous ideas could be spread out instantly. Kierkegaard wrote, "Suppose someone invented an instrument, a convenient little talking tube, which could be heard over the whole land. I wonder if the police would forbid it, fearing that the whole country would become mentally deranged if it were used."

He was more right than he could ever have imagined. Not only convenient little talking tubes, but television and the Internet have sent their tentacles into practically every reach of our society. As I write this in 2001, even broadcast television during so-called "family viewing" hours is filled with so-called reality shows, making entertainment out of embarrassing, humiliating, revolting activities for the sake of ratings. Contestants on these shows win money by having buckets of live rats poured over them, or by having illicit sex just off camera and then telling how it makes them feel.

As the standards of decency creep ever lower, we seem more mesmerized by television than ever. Even as far back as 1977, an experiment in Detroit concluded that when cut off from TV, adults and children experience "symptoms similar to drug withdrawal." In fact, the original experiment had to be modified after 120 households were offered $500 each to participate in the experiment by giving up television for 30 days. Only 27 accepted. The rest turned down $500 rather than do without TV for one month.

It's interesting to me that the debate continues over whether TV is a cause of our behavior as a society or just a reflection of it. Network executives and program producers constantly reassure us that their shows are an eye on the world, not an influencer of it. I'd say the question was settled long ago by the hundreds of millions of dollars that have been spent on television advertising and that continue to be spent at this very moment. If television didn't influence people's behavior, I can guarantee you advertisers wouldn't pay the money they do to advertise their products on it. While the TV hierarchy is telling concerned parents viewing TV won't pervert their children, at the same time they're hawking it to advertisers as a proven persuader that bends viewers to adopt its point of view, whether it's to buy a new car or accept as normal a new form of sexual perversion.

WOULDN'T MORE MONEY FIX OUR SOCIAL PROBLEMS BETTER THAN MORE MORALIZING?

Fathers and mothers are too willing to let the world have its way with their families. There was a time when the head of a household guided his family in a different direction because his faith, along with widely accepted standards of morality, made that direction clear. Too often now, without the guidance of faith, the family has all but ceased to function in a nurturing, moralizing way and that has led to the present downward spiral in standards of behavior and respect for the law.

No amount of welfare spending in the world can fix this problem. Since the advent of large-scale welfare programs beginning with President Johnson's Great Society initiatives in the 1960s, we have spent something like five *trillion* dollars on welfare. If money could repair our broken society, it would have been fixed long before now.

Government is powerless to stop America's decline, but Christian families are not. As Christians we must recognize the family's absolute indispensability. Nothing can replace the family as the nurturing environment for healthy human growth and emotional and spiritual development. We face a crisis of the mind, of the heart, and of the spirit. We must do the right thing with the right motive to turn the trend around.

Even as secularists, naturalists, agnostics, and pagans lament the horrible state of the culture, they defend the very attitudes and practices that have produced it. The Bible makes the relationship between faith and morality crystal clear: "Israel has rejected what is good; an enemy will pursue him. They set up kings without my consent; they choose princes without my approval. With their silver and gold they make idols for themselves. . . . They sow the wind and reap the whirlwind. . . . Israel has forgotten his Maker and built palaces; Judah has fortified many towns. But I will send fire upon their cities that will consume their fortresses" (Hos. 8:3–4, 7, 14).

What our culture needs to regain its former decency is more involvement by Christians and Christian institutions in general, and Christian families in particular. Christian families—those Pilgrims who came from England by way of Holland—were some of the first permanent settlers in the New World; more than 150 years later the American Declaration of Independence was justified by the freedoms to which colonists felt entitled by "nature's God," endowed as they were by their "Creator with certain unalienable rights." Motivated by a belief in anything less, I feel certain the fight for independence would have been lost.

How can Christians be salt and light in politics yet preserve the "wall of separation" between church and state?

Church-state separation was never intended by our fore-bears to mean that people of religious conviction were some-how disqualified from bringing their beliefs to bear on the great public issues of the day. In fact, the whole story of the "wall of separation" between church and state that Thomas Jefferson wrote about in a letter, which has been used to jus-tify every manner of exclusion of religion from public life, has gotten hopelessly scrambled in contemporary discussion and debate. Because it's so important, let's take a minute to unscramble it.

John Leland was a leading Baptist evangelist in colonial America. After preaching in Virginia for twenty years, he returned to his native Massachusetts in 1791 when it became clear that Virginia was not going to do away with slavery as he had hoped. As a leader of the Baptists, Leland opposed rat-ification of the Constitution because he feared it would create a federal, tax-supported church. Nine of the original thirteen states had tax-supported churches, and all of them, whether Episcopalian in the South, Congregationalist in New England, or Presbyterian in between, discriminated against Baptists and other dissenters from the state's "official" faith.

To allay Leland's fears of national discrimination against Baptists, James Madison, a Virginia congressman and later our fourth President, offered him a deal. If Leland would rally

Baptists in support of the Constitution, Madison would do what he could to introduce an amendment that would say Congress would make no law effecting an establishment of religion, and that there would be no governmental interference with the free exercise of religion. Leland agreed, the Constitution was ratified, and Madison's amendment soon became the glorious First Amendment, stating that "Congress shall make no law respecting an establishment of religion, or prohibiting the free exercise thereof."

On New Year's Day, 1802, Leland called on President Thomas Jefferson at the Executive Mansion in Washington to present him with a gift of 600 pounds of cheese from the citizens of western Massachusetts—assuring the president that "no Federalist cows contributed milk for this cheese, only Democratic cows." While at the presidential residence, Leland prayed for God's blessing on Jefferson. That very afternoon, Jefferson wrote his famous letter to the Danbury Baptist Association in Connecticut, which said in part:

> Believing with you that religion is a matter which lies solely between man and his God, that he owes account to none other for his faith or his worship, that the legislative powers of government reach actions only, and not opinions, I contemplate with sovereign reverence that act of the whole American people which declared that their legislature should 'make no law respecting an establishment of religion, or prohibiting the free exercise thereof,' thus building a wall of separation between Church and State.

That was on a Friday. The next Sunday morning, President Jefferson went to a worship service in the House of Representatives chamber at the Capitol and heard John Leland preach. In other words, on January 1 he wrote about the wall of separation and on January 3 he sat in the front row as a Baptist preacher preached a sermon in the House chamber. Clearly Jefferson had no intention of suggesting, ten years after the First Amendment was ratified, that "a wall of separation between Church and State" meant religion should be separated or excluded from government or public life. And neither should we.

But wasn't the whole point of the First Amendment to keep religion out of politics?

Supreme Court Justice Potter Stewart, whose time on the Court (1958–1981) spanned the most cataclysmic years of social change in our history, reaffirmed Jefferson's point of view: "What our Constitution indispensably protects is the freedom of each of us, be he Jew or Agnostic, Christian or Atheist, Buddhist or free thinker, to believe or disbelieve, to worship or not to worship, to pray or keep silent, according to his own conscience, uncoerced and unrestrained by government."

Even *Time* magazine has raised the question in a cover story: "One Nation Under God: has the separation of church and state gone too far?" Amazingly, their answer was yes. They explained:

> For God to be kept out of the classroom or out of America's public debate by nervous school administrators or over-cautious politicians serves no one's interest. That restriction prevents people from drawing on the country's rich and diverse religious heritage for guidance, and it degrades the nation's moral discourse by placing a whole realm of theological reasoning out of

bounds. The price of that sort of quarantine, at a time of moral dislocation, is—and has been—far too high. The courts need to find a better balance between separation and accommodation, and Americans need to respect the new religious freedom they would gain as a result.

America's founders believed not in freedom *from* religion, but freedom *for* religion. The First Amendment was never intended to keep religion out of public policy, but to keep government out of religion.

That's a position Christians have to reclaim, regardless of what a small but vocal minority of people think. People of faith have to step up and be heard when constitutional radicals try to convince us that religious speech is not protected by the First Amendment. If God's name taken in vain is protected speech, even if it's offensive to believers, then God's name invoked in public prayer is surely protected speech, even if it's offensive to non-believers. And you and I need to insist on it.

Nonbelievers, I hate to disappoint you, but there's nothing in the First Amendment that protects you from being offended.

John Adams, vice president under Washington and his successor as president, said in 1798, "We have no government armed in power capable of contending in human passions unbridled by morality and religion. Our Constitution was made for a moral and religious people. It is wholly inadequate for the government of any other." Every state government and city council in the country ought to have that read into the record before every meeting. We must assert our right as Christians to be involved in the moral debate that is all around us. Censorship *of* religion, not *by* religion, is by far the most pervasive form of censorship being practiced in this country today.

What that censorship does is separate the moral principles upon which our nation was founded from the laws and practices and policies they were (according to Adams and Jefferson) supposed to control. If the Constitution is "wholly inadequate" for a nation that has disconnected its government from moral and religious standards, we are in a heap of trouble. Everywhere we take a moral stand, we're challenged by the response, "Whose morality? Yours or mine?" America was founded on Judeo-Christian moral absolutes. America will flounder without them.

DON'T CIVIL RIGHTS LAWS DEPEND ON MORAL ABSOLUTES OF RACIAL EQUALITY?

Those who think Christians shouldn't take part in public debate over values will find that issue and much of the rest of American history incomprehensible. While Martin Luther King Jr. had a dream that people would "be judged not by the color of their skin but by the content of their character," the American Civil Liberties Union fights at every opportunity for the eradication of character valuation from public discourse.

In the 1960s, "You can't legislate morality" once equaled "We don't want civil rights laws." Now it equals "We don't want restrictions on abortion." Laws against murder and rape and stealing legislate morality. Civil rights laws legislate morality; justification for them was rooted in the moral obligation to treat blacks and whites the same under law.

Christian families must speak out against the wicked double standard that applauds moral strength when it opposes apartheid and segregation but condemns it when it opposes abortion. The same churches and denominations that were applauded for taking a stand on civil rights now castigate others for standing fast against abortion. Here's something for the media and cultural elites to chew on: Be honest; it's not our involvement you don't like, it's our position. Quit trying to hide behind the First Amendment.

DOESN'T THE SUCCESS OF MODERN AMERICA
PROVE THAT MORAL ABSOLUTES
ARE UNNECESSARY?

Years ago Carl F. H. Henry observed that twentieth-century philosophies have succumbed to man-centered rather than God-centered focus and orientation. Man rather than God defines truth and goodness in most contemporary universities: "the greatest overturn of ideas and ideals in the history of human thought . . . [that] assumes the comprehensive contingency of everything, including God; the total temporality of all things; the radical relativity of all human thought and life; and the absolute autonomy of man." Obviously, Christianity has become marginalized.

In words that should haunt every thinking Christian, Henry wrote of "a multitude of seething and tormented minds" who "speak now and then of right and wrong, but never of absolutes. They live in a world no longer sure of definitions. Some occasionally churn up the vocabulary of values, but their values take on the sense of mere wants and desires."

This recalls the account in Romans 1:21–28: "For though they knew God, they did not glorify Him as God or show gratitude. Instead, their thinking became nonsense, and their senseless minds were darkened. Claiming to be wise, they became fools and exchanged the glory of the immortal God for images resembling mortal man . . . Therefore God delivered them over in the cravings of their hearts . . . God delivered them over to degrading passions. . . . God delivered them over to a worthless mind. . . ."

One twentieth-century philosopher observed the irony that "when men cease to believe in God, it is not that they believe in nothing. They believe in anything." Believers in anything would never have uprooted their families from England and Holland to start a new life thousands of treacherous miles from home. Believers in anything would never have pledged their lives, fortunes, and sacred honor to rebel against the greatest power in the world—something no colony had ever successfully done up to that time. Believers in anything would never have gone sixteen million strong to fight for their country and for freedom in World War II.

Believers in anything can't keep America going for long, but Christian families can.

HOW SHOULD I BE THINKING ABOUT CHRISTIANITY IN THE CULTURE?

We've got to hold fast to the realization that, now as in times past, Christianity is an utterly radical idea. We must recover a comprehensive understanding of Christian truth and its applicability to every area of life.

Furthermore, to change lives we must first be changed. We must pray for and experience spiritual regeneration, then recognize and accept our responsibilities as Christians to be salt and light. Christ explained the concept in His Sermon on the Mount: "You are the salt of the earth. But if the salt should lose its taste, how can it be made salty? It's no longer good for anything but to be thrown out and trampled on by men. You are the light of the world. A city situated on a hill cannot be hidden. No one lights a lamp and puts it under a basket, but rather on a lampstand, and it gives light for all who are in the

house. In the same way, let your light shine before men, so that
they may see your good works and give glory to your Father
in heaven" (Matt. 5:13–16).

Salt is a disinfectant and preservative. We have to disinfect
and preserve moral standards the way salt does food. We also
have to know firmly and clearly what our standards are and
why we believe in them: salt must remain pure or it loses its
effectiveness. If we're going to have faith in practice, we've got
to get the faith right first.

Light has to shine before men to be seen and be useful.
Knowing the truth is important, but it won't change anything
in the culture. One way or another, Christians naturally shine
out into the world. As Martyn Lloyd-Jones says, "The true
Christian cannot be hid, he cannot escape notice." He will
stand out like "a candle set upon a candlestick." We have to
apply our Christian principles to those things in our culture
that are tearing families apart: pornography, sexual crimes,
promiscuity, sexually transmitted diseases, abortion.

HOW CAN I MAKE A DIFFERENCE
FOR CHRIST RIGHT NOW?

There are plenty of ways you can make a difference in the culture immediately. The Bible is filled with reminders of the
ubiquity of sin:

> We all, like sheep, have gone astray, each of us has
> turned to his own way (Isa. 53:6).
>
> The heart is deceitful above all things and beyond
> cure (Jer. 17:9).
>
> For all have sinned and fall short of the glory of God
> (Rom. 3:23).

When Christians are fulfilling their commission to be salt and light they'll provoke two responses from the world. One is that they will irritate the world. Salt is a preservative and cleanser, but it also stings and irritates. The second response is the fulfillment of God's promise that at least some in the world will see our good works and glorify Him as a result and that our saltiness will create a thirst for purpose and meaning that only God can fulfill.

It may seem like changing the culture for Christ is an impossible task. But remember, nothing is impossible if God wants it to happen. Do all you can, and God will take care of the rest.

Once a young boy went along the beach at low tide, busily scooping up stranded starfish and throwing them back in the surf.

"You can't save all the starfish," his mother yelled. "It doesn't matter."

"It matters to this one," the boy said smiling, holding a starfish aloft in his hand before tossing it back toward the water. Take care of what you can. You can't save everyone, but we each can do something and together we can do a lot.

The greatest journey begins with the first step; the re-establishment of true Christian standards begins with a vision in the hearts and homes of Christian families. "Where there is no vision, the people perish" (Prov. 29:18 KJV). We must proclaim God's changeless standard of truth, holding up the plumb line of God's moral standard to inform, exhort, and convict the people of their desperate need for repentance, regeneration, and revival.

So put on the whole armor of God and get ready to rumble. Brothers and sisters in Christ, "Let's roll."

CHAPTER 3

IN PRAISE OF GOD'S FAMILY PLAN

WHEN IT COMES TO DEFINING THE IDEAL
FAMILY, NOTHING BEATS THE ORIGINAL.

The level of denial secularists express when they come face-to-face with the success of biblically based families is absolutely mind-boggling. These are families ordained by God as the foundational institution of human society and consist of people related to each other by marriage, blood, or adoption. Compared with the modern, all-inclusive definition of a family as anybody living with anybody else, such families are under attack from every quarter of popular culture as backward, restrictive, oppressive, and out of date. Yet these families are the happiest, best adjusted, wealthiest, most law-abiding people in America. Maybe, just maybe, God knew what He was doing after all.

The Bible tells us that God created the world and then created a family to manage significant parts of it according to His direction. He started with Adam and gave him dominion over everything else. Soon afterward, He created Eve out of Adam, because it was not good for man to be alone, and established the foundational God-ordained family: one man and one woman joined together in the sight of God, and then in His time, their children.

According to the Bible, then, faithful spouses and their off-spring are in charge of things. Once again, this isn't my idea but God's: sons of Adam and their families have the privilege and responsibility of managing everything else on earth. Among a Christian family's first duties is to make sure it understands what a family is in the biblical sense and how it must oppose determined and relentless efforts to redefine the family for selfish ends. (By the way, if being in a family is no big deal according to some social commentators and policy-makers, why does everybody want to recast the definition so they can be in one?)

CAN A SINGLE MOM RAISE CHILDREN AS SUCCESSFULLY AS A TWO-PARENT FAMILY?

One of the most damaging contemporary myths about families is that fathers are an option. In some parts of some cities—Harlem in New York City, for example—an estimated 90 percent of children are born out of wedlock. Rather than try to deal with the complex causes of this tragedy and reverse the trend, government organizations often accept the fatherless household as the norm. The result is that one fatherless generation produces another: men have no sense of responsibility for their children, who are raised by unemployed mothers on government assistance or by their grandmothers while their mothers work.

Well-intentioned welfare workers often compound the problem when they perpetuate the myth that these lifestyles are just as good as any. These authority figures have given welfare children the tragically false notion that, as one little girl said cheerfully, "I don't need no daddy!"

Not only is this perspective completely at odds with Christian teaching and tradition, it is incredibly expensive in terms of the literally millions of children who live poor, neglected lives, and too often who go through life with their spiritual and emotional needs unmet. Rather than becoming productive, contributing members of society, they subsist on welfare indefinitely and drain away public resources that have to be spent on crime prevention, police protection, prisons, courts, and other somber evidence of families gone awry, rather than on schools, parks, libraries, and museums.

HOW CAN CHRISTIANS CONVINCE NON-CHRISTIANS THAT BIBLE-BASED MARRIAGE IS BEST?

Christians can see that there's a tremendous spiritual cost to the secular redefinition of the family away from biblical standards. But everybody—Christian, druid, or cat worshiper—should recognize there are also tremendous social, material, and financial costs. As an extension of God's common grace, even the most avowed non-Christian would benefit from a resurgence of interest in traditional Christian marriage.

Steven E. Rhoads made this point convincingly in an article for *The American Enterprise* entitled, "The Case Against Androgynous Marriage": "Fathers matter," Rhoads asserts, "because fathers help boys become responsible men and teach girls good men will love them even if they don't 'put out.' When men who've been good fathers get a divorce, they usually divorce their children too."

God made Adam the head of the household. It is the man's natural position, whether the world—or the man—chooses to recognize it or not. Rhoads continues: "Feminists denounced the idea of biblical submission as 'domestic feudalism.' Most people don't care. Women go to law school and men wear earrings. But social science research on intact marriages finds that in real marriages, male headship is simply a fact. . . ." Rhoads continues, "If we care about marriages that work, the Baptists just may have something to teach us."

We Southern Baptists get a lot of heat from the public and the media for our denominational stance on family issues. We're "repressive" and "sexist" and "out of touch with the times." But what we endorse comes straight from the Bible: the man is to be the head of the house, yet he is commanded to lead and protect and safeguard his wife and family—to love selflessly and sacrificially as Christ loves the church. I'd say that makes Christianity the protector of women rather than an exploiter of them. The idea of women being submissive to men is as old as history; however, the idea of men being responsible and accountable to women is a radical, specifically Christian concept.

The primary emphasis in the apostle Paul's Ephesian epistle is on the husband's responsibility to serve his wife by loving her "as Christ loved the church." How did Christ love the church? The love with which Christ loved the church was the *agape* love that He modeled by giving His life for the church. It is *agape* love which transforms worldly ideas of submission from dominance and subservience to humility and service.

In writing to the Corinthian church, Paul penned a divinely inspired essay on this *agape* love with which husbands are commanded to love their wives: "Love is patient and kind, Love is not jealous or boastful or proud or rude. Love does not demand its own way. Love is not irritable, and it keeps no record of when it has been wronged. It is never glad about injustice. . . . Love never gives up, never loses faith, is always hopeful, and endures through every circumstance. Love will last forever. . . ." (1 Cor. 13:4–8a NLT). *Agape* love requires the husband to *always* put his wife's needs above his own and to give himself in self-sacrificial service to her.

IF THE MAN IS THE HEAD OF THE HOUSEHOLD, HOW CAN MEN AND WOMEN BE EQUAL?

It's often misunderstood or ignored, but the point is that since the husband and wife are both created in the image of God, they are of equal worth before God. Just because one of them gets to be the tiebreaker is no indication he is better or superior in God's eyes. The creation of male and female human beings was the crowning moment of the creation process. The gift of gender is thus an essential and inseparable part of God's perfect plan.

Men and women are equal but not identical. And it works. Even skeptics who refuse to accept the superiority of the Christian family on theological or religious grounds have little choice but to accept it on scientific or financial grounds. God's plan works, and works better than any other arrangement, because it is God's plan.

"Feminists can hardly look at married men without a certain measure of disgust," Rhoads writes. "In the typical two-earner family they contribute about half as much housework as their employed wives and less than half as much solo child care.

"Most feminists believe men's power in the home comes from their power in the marketplace. . . . To answer, we need to know whether women's power soars when they are the big earners in a marriage."

Feminists declare that women should have equal opportunity to be the big wage earner in the family. Big paycheck equals big happiness, right? Not exactly. Rhoads tells us that the facts reveal a different story: "When the wife earns more than the husband, neither say the wife's job is more important. A high-earning wife is more likely than other women to leave the labor force or move to a lower position. They try to be especially attractive and sexual; husbands do very little additional housework. One survey of over twenty studies on marital power found that wife-dominated couples were the least happy and that the wives were less happy than their husbands."

Again, these aren't just my opinions, but carefully researched facts, though I agree wholeheartedly with the conclusions. Traditional families headed by a man who is also the principal wage earner are happier and more successful than any other arrangement.

IF MEN AND WOMEN ARE EQUAL, DOESN'T THAT MEAN THEY'RE THE SAME?

Our culture promotes unisex perfume, haircuts, and rest rooms. We hear women have every right to be firefighters and footsoldiers if they want to be. But men and women are different. They are born with gender-specific skills and abilities. These are not forced upon them by a sexist society. And adults are no more interchangeable than their children. Little boys encouraged to play with dolls will soon invent Rambo Barbie; little girls with toy tanks will use them as baby carriages.

If you think men and women are the same, look at how advertisers appeal to them. These experts know how different men and women are because their livelihood depends on it. Men and women watch different shows: daytime dramas advertise makeup; football games advertise cars.

With very rare exceptions, men are wired to be providers and women to be nurturers (though history gives us exceptions, like Amelia Earhart, that prove the rule). That's why splitting the housework fifty-fifty between working spouses so seldom produces a happy result. Even couples where the man does 40 percent of the housework are stressed: the husbands are unhappy, and there is often constant negotiation and compromise over child rearing. Rhoads concludes, "In real life, most women do not seem to want equal worldly power. Even professional women want the man to be the chief provider, not only because they believe the husband's work is more important to his sense of self, but also because they need their husbands to be successful."

Research shows that working women respect stay-at-home moms more than they respect other working mothers. Even the social aspect of working reflects the natural difference between women and men. Men need to be alone to sort through problems while women prefer companionship. A woman might need to spend time in her room. Men would rather get away to the golf course or the fishing hole. They want more time away from home.

Men with real problems need advice or action, not talk. Women, on the other hand, love talking through and exploring all the aspects of an issue. Men only want to talk about a problem when they're working directly on solving it. Talking about a problem they can't fix only leads to stress and frustration.

Furthermore, husbands of white-collar wives with unsupportive bosses are more than three times as likely as others to die of heart disease, apparently as a result of frustration at hearing day in and day out about seemingly unsolvable problems at their wives' jobs. Men don't like to talk about unsolvable problems; women do.

Men can't be reprogrammed to become as communicative and wife-like as women. Testosterone research suggests it's against men's most basic hormonal drives. A study of patients released from the hospital after recovery from congestive heart failure shows that "for women, the absence of emotional support in the community increased their death rates more than eightfold. For men it made no difference at all."

IS THERE ACTUALLY A "MATERNAL INSTINCT," OR DO MEN AND WOMEN HAVE THE SAME NATURAL POTENTIAL FOR NURTURING CHILDREN?

Scientific research reveals that women are genetically programmed to be more interested in interpersonal attachment than men, making them naturally better suited for raising children. In almost all cultures and household groups, babies are cared for by their mothers—even in communal situations and primitive cultures. Of course there are exceptions once again that prove the rule. Some women, Rhoads reports, find child care "boring and depressing. But most do not. In her powerful defense of homemakers, *Domestic Tranquillity,* Carolyn Graglia describes her child-rearing days as an 'everyday epiphany of exquisite happiness.'"

Conversely, women facing the prospect of going childless suffer deep-seated physical distress. Female patients undergoing infertility treatments have levels of depression comparable to patients with AIDS and cancer.

Rhoads reports other specific chemical characteristics that differentiate the natural tendencies of men and women. "Women's estrogen facilitates the effect of oxytocin, a substance which promotes touching, holding, and bonding. During pregnancy and nursing oxytocin surges in women, engendering pleasure and relaxation. When male rats are given oxytocin, they start building nests like their sisters."

A mother's voice, which the baby has heard in utero, slows, calms, and steadies a baby's heart. A father's voice doesn't have the same effect. In fact, some male voices frighten young children. Time and again the plain fact is that fathers and mothers are not identical pop-in puzzle pieces. Each has a set of innate skills. Together as man and wife they supply all a child's needs.

The maternal instinct is unique to women, and that makes it all the more frustrating that our society has marginalized motherhood to the point where we practically demand that mothers work as wage earners. Our society covets wealth and the trappings of wealth—two new cars, a sleek motorboat, a vacation cabin—and looks down its nose at women who feel their place is at home with their children and want to be appreciated and accepted for it. Working women build retirement benefits and social security; they have tax benefits, insurance coverage, and paid vacations while stay-at-home women have no comparable financial reward.

WHAT REAL PROOF IS THERE THAT MOTHERS AND FATHERS AREN'T INTERCHANGEABLE?

Hard research data point to the fact that men and women are not interchangeable as heads of the household or nurturers of children, nor interchangeable as authority figures or breadwinners. Secular studies show that 61 percent of husbands work more than forty hours per week while 24 percent of wives do. Husbands are seven times as likely as wives to work sixty hours per week or more. Fifty-one percent of mothers work full time, but only 30 percent of full-time working mothers want to work full time. "These figures do not point to an androgynous future, and if we want strong marriages we should be delighted," Rhoads says.

Women divorce men who don't work steadily at good jobs; men divorce women when they fail as homemakers. Men are dominant; women are peacemakers. Women give in during arguments more than men; family distress affects them more. Their perceived failure as a wife can't be offset by success elsewhere. "When wives perceive their family and marriage are not going well, their blood pressure goes up," Rhoads reports. "When husbands perceive trouble, their blood pressure does not go up, but the husbands' perception of trouble will send the wives' blood pressure up."

"Studies show that the more housework men do, the less they love their wives, and the more arguments the couple has," Rhoads concludes. Is this selfishness? No, because it isn't that the man is lazy, it's that he's doing work he isn't wired to do. He could do other work that's just as hard, or harder, and be far more content.

Does that mean "a woman's place is in the home" and nowhere else?

This doesn't necessarily mean every woman's place is in the kitchen all day every day. There are plenty of biblical examples of women working outside the home. The "virtuous woman" of Proverbs 31 works with her hands, buys property, invests her earnings prudently, gives to the poor, and "senses that her gain is good" (v. 18 NASB). Until the rapid industrialization of America after World War I, most women did a lot more than keep the kids clean and cook supper on the stove. In 1920, 70 percent of Americans lived on farms where women tended livestock, raised chickens, collected eggs, churned butter, pieced quilts, and much more while their husbands worked in the fields.

The stay-at-home mom, personified by June Cleaver in the classic 1950s TV show *Leave It to Beaver,* was actually a product of the previous decade when the men came home from fighting World War II and women left their factory jobs for a long delayed season of marriage and motherhood.

As long as her God, her husband, and her children come first, there's nothing inherently wrong with women working. (My wife, a marriage and family therapist I met in seminary where we both were responding to God's call to full-time Christian service, works outside the house and has since our youngest child was in kindergarten.) The problem, if it comes, lies in the reason why she works. Is it a special calling of God's will for her life? Is it a ministry? Is it in the name of Christian education?

Does she need to work? Is she a widow, or is her husband unable to support his family through no fault of his own? Do they have a large family? Are there dependent elder parents or other relatives in the household? Large medical or educational expenses?

These would all be good reasons for a woman to work outside the home under some—but not all—conditions. Are there small children at home? How many and how young? By working, is she slighting them? What about her husband? Does he agree that the wife working is in the family's best interest? If not, the wife should not work.

HOW DOES MARRIAGE AFFECT THE CRIME RATE?

From early adolescence, single males show a statistically much higher rate of criminal and antisocial behavior than women. The best cure, according to exhaustive documentation, is marriage. Single men commit nearly 90 percent of the crimes in the

United States every year. Marriage is good for society, as
Rhoads points out, "because it gets single men off the street."

David Courtwright's book *Violent Land* shows how violence, death, and exploitation have followed unmarried men in
all locales throughout American history. "Marriage is good for
children because intact families fight crime, illegitimacy,
depression, drugs, and school failure. And marriage is good
for both spouses; married persons are healthier, wealthier, and
happier than single folk."

Men are programmed to dominate. Up to a certain point,
this domination is essential for effective leadership. But over-
domination leads to problems of its own—domestic abuse, for
example. How then do we encourage male leadership while
insisting on restraint? The secular world is befuddled by this
dilemma. We train soldiers to be tough and ruthless—characteristics that are essential for them to succeed—then are
appalled by what they do sometimes as a result of that
toughness.

The secular world is stumped because the only workable
answer is a spiritual answer. We have to remind tough, dominant, aggressive leaders of what Rhoads recognizes as their
"sacred obligation to use their familial power to serve their
families." There is such a thing as *sacred obligation*. Husbands
must be ready to sacrifice themselves for their wives and children as Christ gave all for the church.

WHAT WILL A TRADITIONAL MARRIAGE DO FOR MY SEX LIFE?

By making the male role in marriage vital, incidentally,
Christians attract more men to it. And by condemning extramarital sex, we can make alternatives to marriage less attractive
and less available.

One recent study found that "the most satisfied husbands were those who believed they had the greater decision-making power even where there was no independent evidence of it." Men want to make the decisions even if they say otherwise on the surface.

Rhoads quotes a memorable example. "Women in such marriages probably rule indirectly as the wisest wives usually do. David Blankenhorn tells the tale of a traditional wife who said her husband was the head of the family and she was the neck—which turns the head in the direction it should go. Most wives set husbands going in better directions, and civilization is in their debt.

"The facts contradict feminist doctrine on women's route to marital power and happiness . . . the husbands most likely to help wives with household chores are orthodox Christians."

Respect for and acknowledgment of traditional marriage roles will even improve your sex life. Rhoads writes, "Still another large study on sexuality has found that the women most likely to achieve orgasm each and every time are conservative Protestants. So if we put it all together, it looks as if the more traditional and religious woman, far from being a serf in 'domestic feudalism,' is the most likely to have a mate who shares housework and satisfies her sexually."

No wonder most men who go to Promise Keepers rallies say their wives encouraged them to attend.

WHAT'S THE HARM IN EXPERIMENTING WITH
VARIOUS LIFESTYLES FOR A WHILE
BEFORE I SETTLE DOWN?

Barbara Dafoe Whitehead addresses this issue head-on in her feature article "How We Mate" for *City Journal*.

She begins by noting how marriage has diminished in importance today compared with the past, with the rate dropping by a third between 1960 and 1995. "Marriage no longer looms like Mount Everest on the landscape of adult life," she says. "It is more like a hill that people can choose to climb, up and down, once or twice in a lifetime, or bypass altogether." More and more often, Americans choose an alternative to traditional marriage and family—to their peril.

"Cohabitation, rather than marriage, is the distinctive union of the new mating regime. Almost two thirds of adults born between 1963 and 1974 began with cohabitation rather than marriage, compared with 16 percent of men and 7 percent of women born between the mid-30s and early 40s."

Cohabitation frequently begins with what teens and young adults call a hookup. This is a sexual encounter based predominantly on physical attraction. Sometimes the participants scarcely know each other. In some cases, Whitehead reports, they've never kissed or even held hands before having sex.

> The hookup is a brief sexual relationship with no strings or rings attached. It can be shorter than a one-night stand or longer than a fling. It may lead to a living-together partnership. But sooner or later (usually sooner), the hookup ends in betrayal and abandonment and thus to breakup. The breakup is filled with passion in one or both partners. Leave-taking triggers a torrent of hot emotions—anger, jealousy, hatred—followed by competing fantasies of getting back together or getting even. Finally, the fiery passion subsides and the fantasies fade, leaving behind regret and resentment.

This alternative to marriage seems to be most prevalent "among two socially important and culturally influential groups: the never married young, particularly those on the lower two-thirds of the socioeconomic scale; and blacks of all ages and socioeconomic levels. (Statistically, blacks are single for much of their lives and many of them never marry.)"

Today's teenagers are the first to come of age under the new rules. "They know little of romantic courtship and even less about marriage, having seen so few examples. Gone are friendship rings, double dating, going steady, the slow buildup to the first 'I love you,' and the anticipation of the first kiss. Gone is any reasonable expectation that a sexual relationship carries with it the promise of marriage. Instead, teens party in comradely groups and 'hook up' for sex."

Cohabitation precedes over half of all first marriages today, though it's less common among college-educated individuals. Not only is cohabitation overwhelmingly likely to produce hurt feelings and broken relationships, it's dangerous. Current or former boyfriends commit 51 percent of all violent crime by intimate partners. Cohabitors are almost twice as likely to report hitting, shoving, or throwing as married men and women. Also, households that include a mother and a boyfriend who is not the biological father of the children pose the greatest risk of child abuse of any household combination.

And the news only gets worse. "The hookup-breakup cycle spirals downward. Each successive relationship starts out at a lower level of trust and commitment than the one before. Lower commitment leads to cheating. Cheating to lying, lying to mistrust, mistrust to breakup. And mistrust is almost inevitable, since the hookup-breakup mating regime is so often based on a lie. It requires women to feign a lack of interest in marriage in order to 'keep a guy.' . . . Since the new regime rewards women for their lack of pickiness about partners, little wonder that we see a growing crowd of estimable women who unerringly fall into bed with losers and louts."

WHAT'S THE RESULT OF OUR GROWING POPULATION OF NEVER-MARRIED MOMS?

Men have always liked remaining unmarried. As countless mothers have told their wanton daughters over the generations, "Why should your boyfriend buy the cow if he can get the milk for free?" The difference these days is that women are accepting single life more than ever. There are two reasons for this. First, because of women's growing economic independence; and second, the growing belief in American society that a woman has the right to raise a baby on her own.

One surprise of the sexual revolution of our time, especially for feminists, is that even unmarried women want babies. "A baby," Whitehead declares, "is the trophy women most prize."

Birth control and legal abortion liberated women from unwanted pregnancy and men from unwanted marriage. They have also dramatically increased pressure on women to have sex without promise or expectation of marriage. This is convenient for the man because it gives him sex without the burden of marriage, and it's handy for the woman because she can have a child without all the bother of a husband. But the result for everyone involved—particularly the children born out of wedlock themselves and society at large—is disaster.

As soon as the sons of single mothers start "acting like boys," reports Whitehead, the mothers "start looking for a man. A social worker in a wealthy suburb of Boston reports that the mothers most urgently seeking male mentors for their sons are well-educated, single-mothers-by-choice whose darling baby boys have grown into rage-filled teenagers."

The overall picture of the popular secular alternative to "domestic feudalism" is bleak. "The new regime's effects on children are unambiguous. It leaves them with family attachments that are shifting and insecure. . . . Fully 3/4 of children born to cohabiting parents will see the partnership break up before they reach age sixteen. Only a third of children born to married couples face a similar fate."

Children have become, in Whitehead's words, "the hostages and victims of intimate warfare. . . . The new mating regime—which began with the promise of enlarged happiness for all—generates a superabundance of discontent, pain, and misery, something that should be a matter of concern to a society as solicitous of adult psychological well-being as ours."

WHAT'S THE LIBERAL ESTABLISHMENT RESPONSE TO OVERWHELMING PROOF THAT BIBLICAL FAMILIES ARE BEST?

Look at the results of the National Marriage Project at Rutgers University called "The State of Our Unions—The Social Health of Marriage in America." Having graduated from an Ivy League school myself, I can assure you that the eastern higher education establishment—a bastion of secular liberalism—would do nothing to promote conservative Christianity unless they had absolutely no choice. But look at their analysis.

> As an institution, marriage has lost much of its legal, religious and social meaning and authority. It has dwindled to a 'couples relationship,' mainly designed for the sexual and emotional gratification of each adult. . . . some elites seem to believe that support for marriage is synonymous with far-right political or religious views,

discrimination against single parents, and tolerance of domestic violence.

At the national policy level, marriage has received remarkably little bipartisan study or attention. During a four-decade period of dramatic historic change in marriage, no national studies, government commissions or task forces have been set up to examine the status of marriage or to propose measures to strengthen it.

Even the eastern establishment knows something is wrong in the world and that something has to be done about it. If Rutgers be for us, who can be against us?

And so we see that the biblical view of marriage has undergone a scathing attack from the popular culture and image makers over the past generation. But at the same time, one research project after another reveals that God's version of marriage and family works better than anything else. God knew what He was doing after all. The closer to the biblical standard a family is, the safer, wealthier, and happier its members will be. The further it strays from that biblical ideal, the more likely it is to fail.

Are you worried about being labeled a prude? Don't ever be afraid to defend the Christian ideal of marriage. It is the most successful by every measure; furthermore, it's God's plan. But you don't have to use a religious argument to win your case. To people who refuse the Gospel of Christ, the spiritual argument will fall on deaf ears. But thanks to God's common grace, even the lost can be persuaded—by an appeal to their self-interest in money, safety, and happiness—that God's way is best, even if they don't recognize it as that.

CHAPTER 4

ASKING FOR CHAOS

According to the 2000 census, the number of households headed by unmarried people grew almost 72 percent in the previous ten years. Illegitimate births made up 3.8 percent of births in 1940; in 2000, a third of all American children were born out of wedlock. As we've seen, children from single-parent families suffer in every quality-of-life category compared with children of married parents. They are poorer, sicker, more inclined to crime; they are people of unfulfilled potential and lost opportunity; and their hope of spiritual fulfillment is dim.

Families don't get the support they need in the public policy arena. The leaders responsible for founding America and guiding it through the past two and a half centuries—leaders responsible for crafting the freest, richest, most powerful nation in the history of the world—were almost all operating from either a Judeo-Christian worldview or, later, from what Francis Schaeffer called a "Christian memory." The vast majority of them claimed identification with a Protestant denomination. This isn't jingoism or discrimination, just historical fact. If they had answered, "So what?" to issues of faith at any time of crisis, I believe it's safe to say there would be no United States today. Since the Pilgrims, Judeo-Christian values and morality have been absolutely essential to America's health and success.

IF BIBLICAL FAMILIES ARE SO GOOD FOR OUR COUNTRY, WHERE ARE ALL THEIR FRIENDS IN CONGRESS?

If more biblical families would increase productivity, reduce crime, and lessen the strain on social services, you'd think people would be crawling out of the woodwork to encourage people in that direction. But they don't. Why?

James Dobson notes political figures and candidates seldom mention marriage because the God-inspired institution of the family "has become politically incorrect. It is reviled as offensive to those living together out of wedlock and to some homosexual activists."

Should the government endorse homosexual marriage? What about the claim of freedom and liberty in the name of "nature and nature's God" in the Declaration of Independence? Whether you approve of homosexual relations or not, it's clear that it is not in line with nature and nature's God. In fact, until fairly recently the euphemism in polite company for homosexual acts was "unnatural acts." I agree with Dr. Dobson, who says that if the idea of homosexual or communal marriage "takes root, the institution of marriage will be finished."

A recent study quoted by Maggie Gallagher in *National Review* suggests it's essential that everyone—Christian and non-Christian alike—understand the social cost of never-married mothers, divorce, and all the rest. "Activists realize," she says, "that welfare reform succeeded only when Americans realized that welfare dependence hurt not only taxpayers, but the poor as well. Similarly, the efforts to reduce divorce and

unwed childbearing will succeed only when Americans understand that the goal is not the narrow one of imposing legal
punishment for sexual immorality, but the broader strengthening of marriage as a positive social force."

According to the study, even after variations in race, income,
and cognitive ability had been factored out, boys raised outside of intact marriages are two to three times more likely to
be incarcerated than those in households that meet the traditional, biblical definition of a family. Again, Christian precepts
lead to secular benefits. Good living and Christian living are
inseparable.

There's even hope for politicians who stand up for traditional marriage. Gallagher continues:

> Politicians who have begun to speak on this issue are
> finding that as long as the focus is on building a better
> future, marriage is a shared aspiration—a value that
> unites, not divides. I've interviewed dozens of single
> mothers, for example, and I've never met one who,
> when asked what she wants for her son, said, "I'd like
> him to impregnate his girlfriend and then move a hun-
> dred miles away." . . . Nobody marries hoping to end
> up divorced, and nobody, in the privacy of her heart,
> dreams of the day her daughter will become a single
> parent.

WHAT CONVINCING PROOF IS THERE THAT SINGLE MOTHERHOOD IS A FAILURE?

Women making the conscious decision to be single mothers is
a chaotic trend in our culture. Not long ago the *National
Review* Web site carried a story by Melissa Seckora titled,
"Crash Landing: Is flying solo really what it's made out to

be?" that expanded on the myth of successful single mother-hood. "Single women want to have children, and want to be good mothers—without needing to rely financially on husbands who love and respect them. This," she concludes, "is a *bad* combination, for women and children alike."

Her research shows that at every income level except the highest ($50,000 and above), children with never-married mothers were more likely than children in two-parent households to be expelled, suspended, have emotional problems and exhibit antisocial behavior. They are also more likely to die an accidental death.

Daughters of single parents are 53 percent more likely to marry as teens, 111 percent more likely to have children as teens, 164 percent more likely to give birth prematurely, and 92 percent more likely to file for divorce. One forensic psychologist said, "The one human being most capable of curbing the antisocial aggression of a boy is his biological father." Sen. Daniel Patrick Moynihan—whom I can't say I agree with all that often—got it exactly right when he said, "A community that allows a large number of young men to grow up in broken families, dominated by women, never acquiring any stable relationship to male authority, never acquiring any rational expectation about the future—that community asks for and gets chaos."

The Christian media have spent a great deal of time pondering the dilemma of modern marriage standards. An editorial in *Christianity Today* compares modern marriage to a caffeine-free diet cola: "all synthetic substitutions and no substance." Good marriage mirrors Christ's love for the church, not as a theological object lesson but as "a lived-out parable of the principles that undergird the universe."

WHAT CAN I DO TO KEEP
MARRIED COUPLES MARRIED?

There's no telling how much ink and effort have been spent recounting the pitfalls of broken families. It's important to understand the problem and its causes but even more important to take actions to reverse this destructive trend. Certainly there are societal changes taking place that encourage the breakup and distortion of families. Still, Christians could do a lot more to preserve the institution of traditional marriage.

It's up to us, our clergy, and our church leadership to hold marriage partners accountable for their behavior and to compel husbands and wives to realize that marriage vows represent an unconditional lifetime promise. Marriage is forever, regardless of what pop culture says.

Writing in *World* magazine, Joel Belz speaks for many Christians when he admits, "It's easy to blame the bad guys—the terribly secularized media, Hollywood, the public schools, the demands of big business—but maybe the biggest blame rests on God's own people. . . . the picture we in fact offer is barely distinguishable from that offered by the rest of society."

It isn't easy or comfortable to hold a brother or sister in Christ accountable for their marital behavior, but it's our duty. Nobody ever said being a Christian was easy. Belz looks at three specific ways Christians can strengthen the institution of marriage:

1. *Resist divorce.* Obvious as it is, this option is overlooked more often than not. Friends and church members hear that a couple is splitting up, and their reaction is usually, "Isn't that too bad!" when it should be, "No way!" Church officers must be willing to use their God-given authority to persuade and encourage people to remain married.

2. *Identify the guilty party and hold him accountable.*
Matthew 19 is explicit in laying out the only biblical foundation for divorce: "And I tell you, whoever divorces his wife, except for sexual immorality, and marries another, commits adultery" (Matt. 19:9). Only unfaithfulness or irreconcilable desertion by a non-Christian spouse (1 Cor. 7:12–15) provides biblical justification for divorce. For Christians, marriage is pronounced by the church and should be dissolved only under the discipline of the church; the church is obliged to uncover the truth.

3. *Understand the circumstances surrounding the divorce of a prospective member.* Churches that want to discourage divorce must be careful on what terms they welcome as members those who carry the guilt for breaking up previous marriages.

HOW HAVE PASTORS CONTRIBUTED TO THE GROWING FAILURE RATE OF MARRIAGES?

Something I wonder about as a pastor who has had the honor of officiating at numerous marriage ceremonies is why Christian ministers perform some of the marriages they do. I believe there are people married in the church every day who don't understand their marriage vows, who don't realize the lifetime nature of the marriage commitment, and who don't approach their roles as husband and wife in a biblical manner because they have no idea in the world what that means. Some of them aren't even professing Christians. There's nothing to stop these people from getting married by a judge or justice of the peace, but responsible Christian pastors have no business marrying them until the pastor is convinced they understand what the whole process means and that they understand the divinely ordained obligations they assume in being joined in "holy" matrimony.

The United States has the highest divorce rate in the world. To understand why, listen to marriage vows. Today's vows tend more and more to be written by the couple themselves and tend to downplay or avoid any pledge of marital permanence. The old vows conformed the couple to the marriage institution; the new ones are a subjective projection. As one commentator puts it, "Rather than the vow creating the couple, the couple creates the vow." Couples "in effect become the gods of their own marriages." Pastors not only allow but encourage couples to be wise in their own eyes, rather than submitting to the teachings of Christ when they allow such practices.

The Baptist Faith and Message statement offers as clear a definition as I've ever heard of marriage as "the uniting of one man and one woman in covenant commitment for a lifetime."

Christians, then, have to hold themselves, their friends, and members of their church to godly standards in marriage. Is this hopelessly old-fashioned? It is old-fashioned, but, far from being hopeless, it's our best hope for reviving traditional marriage.

WHAT'S THE DIVORCE RATE OF BORN-AGAIN CHRISTIANS COMPARED WITH OTHER COUPLES?

Unfortunately, as a group, Christians have to admit that we often want others to do as we say, not as we do. For example, recent studies show virtually no difference between the divorce rate of Christians and the general population.

Roughly 15 percent of senior Protestant pastors are divorced. I'm particularly grieved to learn 29 percent of Baptists are divorced, the highest rate among Christian denominations. Catholics and Lutherans are tied for the lowest rate at 21 percent; more than one of every five clergy marriages ends in divorce.

Is it better for the children to dissolve a bad marriage rather than staying married and miserable?

Judith Wallerstein has conducted one of the longest-running, most in-depth research projects ever about the effects of divorce on children. We'll look at her results in detail later. However for now, consider the fact that she believes the effects on children are so bad that there should be a waiting period before a divorce during which parents have to make long-range plans for their children. The divorcing couple should also be required to undergo counseling and mediation.

Reviewing Wallerstein's work in the *Weekly Standard,* Fred Barnes writes, "Wallerstein challenges the view, dominant since the 1960s, that if parents divorce amicably, the worst their children will suffer is temporary disruption in their lives: The long-term adverse impact will be nil. Since lawyers and counselors and academics created this benign take on divorce in the first place, they have a vested interest in preserving it—which makes Wallerstein their worst nightmare. She is destroying their baby."

Far from being a transient experience, divorce forces children to face "painful consequences that last well into middle age." And—shocker of shockers—Wallerstein concludes, contrary to everything the experts have thrown at us for forty years, that a bad marriage is nevertheless "better than a good divorce as far as the health and welfare of kids are concerned."

By the way, baby boomers (including me and, I expect, many of you), who were doted upon as children, often have proven not to be very good parents. They have been far more prone to divorce, extra-marital sexual immorality, drug use, child neglect, and child abuse than were their own parents' generation.

WHAT'S A COVENANT MARRIAGE, AND WHY SHOULD ANYBODY WANT ONE?

To the credit of their legislatures and the benefit of their citizens, the states of Louisiana and Arizona have come up with a radical and encouraging solution to the national decline in marriage commitment: the option of a covenant marriage. About twenty more states are looking into it. And Governor Frank Keating of Oklahoma questioned why it was easier to get a divorce than a hunting license.

Covenant marriage goes against the idea of "no-fault" divorce by affirming that the couple believes marriage is a commitment for life; that they have chosen to be married and disclosed everything that could adversely affect the decision; that they have received premarital counseling. Furthermore, they promise to get counseling if serious conflict arises in their relationship, and agree in advance to exclusive grounds for divorce—adultery, felony imprisonment, abuse, and a few others.

The fact is that every marriage ought to be taken in this light. But since "regular" marriage has become so devalued, the interest in covenant marriage is encouraging.

Only a small fraction (2 to 3 percent) of couples choose it in the two states where it's available, but a surprising number of married couples are trading up from conventional to covenant relationships. Individuals, families, communities, and the nation will be stronger as a result.

Covenant marriage is a wise public investment in the future. As Alan J. Hawkins of the Family Studies Center School of Family Life, Brigham Young University, observes, "The social and financial costs to local, state, and federal governments of failed marriages and the weakening institution of marriage are staggering. . . . The passage of covenant marriage legislation probably has been facilitated as much by a sense of reducing government expenses and promoting the public welfare as it has by conservative religious sentiments."

Once again, the Christian thing to do is also the economical, beneficial, right thing to do.

Furthermore, "children born in the no-fault divorce era have experienced the problems of their parents' divorces and want to avoid passing those same experiences on to their own children."

Covenant marriage is important for the symbolic power of the law, encouraging counseling, and for specifically stating the moral grounds for a divorce.

WHAT DO DIVORCE LAWYERS SAY ABOUT COVENANT MARRIAGE?

John Crouch is a divorce lawyer who testified before the Maryland House of Delegates as they considered whether to enact covenant marriage legislation.

Witness to many acrimonious breakups over his career, Crouch testified that covenant marriage would be good for people who chose it, people who didn't, and people who weren't even married. He said, "We divorce lawyers see our clients getting more and more alienated from the system, wanting to take vengeance on each other, and getting the kids involved in their crusades against each other. . . . [We tell our clients] divorce is a normal part of life. . . . get over it and start the whole process with someone else . . . But we have been telling people these things for 30 years, and they just seem to be getting worse, madder, more desperate."

Though divorce proceedings provide his livelihood, Crouch admitted that the process and costs are out of control. "A covenant marriage law would restore some sense of control." There would also be protection and security. "Today it hardly makes sense to tie up your whole economic future and emotional well-being in a marriage which has a good chance of not lasting, and people know that."

Covenant marriage gives people the safety and comfort once associated with all marriages. And, in its limited use so far, also keeps some couples whose marriage was probably doomed from the start, from marrying in the first place. (More than 20 percent of couples who have premarital counseling don't get married.)

The connection between traditional Christian marriage and the political and social consequences of self-sufficient families has been highlighted in reports by the Heritage Foundation. Louisiana state legislator Tony Perkins introduced covenant marriage legislation in the summer of 1997. The Heritage Foundation reported: "In a culture that disposes of commitments as easily as paper cups, the very existence of a more muscular marital contract can help redefine attitudes toward marriage." The Foundation called Perkins's action "an object lesson that law can be used to instigate, but not compel, traditional virtue."

Civil law promoting stronger marriages can have a profound effect. History tells us that legislation can influence societal behavior. The most vivid example of our time is the civil rights movement. The laws came first, and public opinion and behavior followed afterward. The same benefit can accrue as the result of covenant legislation.

WHAT'S HAPPENING TO THE DIVORCE RATE
AS WOMEN'S INCOME RISES?

Heritage Foundation research shows that when divorce rates rise, society as a whole faces negative consequences. Patrick F. Fagan, a Heritage Foundation Fellow, says that "marriage is the central institution of society" and should be preserved except in the most dire circumstances. "America has always had the tendency toward the individual. But the sexual revolution added massively and tilted it toward a dysfunctional level. . . . The closer a woman's income becomes equal to the man's, the higher the divorce rate becomes."

His statistical conclusion: faith is the answer. "Religious worship is the great protector, and that is not just an axiom. There are statistics proving it consistently."

The more closely we look at divorce, the more the cost of broken marriages is apparent. Divorced people are sicker. Every kind of cancer kills more divorced than not divorced people. Divorced men are twice as likely to die of cardiovascular disease as married men. Pneumonia is seven times as high in white men and suicide four times higher in divorced versus married men. According to the National Institute of Mental Health, "the single most powerful predictor of stress-related physical as well as emotional illness is marital disruption."

And while the effect on couples is devastating emotionally, physically, and financially, the result on children is even worse. Wallerstein's research exposes as selfish and false the claims that children get over divorce soon and are better off in a single-parent household than with two unhappy parents. Long-term studies indicate that for children, divorce produces emotional trauma that endures for life. More than a million children a year experience divorce firsthand. To them, that translates into profound rejection, abandonment, fear, and anger.

Children of divorced parents are more likely to be victims of abuse, have more health, behavioral, and emotional problems, suffer higher crime and drug abuse rates, and have higher suicide rates. They are statistically poorer performers in school, and more likely to drop out or repeat a grade. Almost 50 percent move into poverty after divorce. For every dollar spent by the government to prevent divorce, $1,000 is spent dealing with the effects of divorce. What a savage, cruel waste of our resources. Preventing divorce—far more than dealing with the aftermath—should be a matter of public health. (Step number 1: get rid of no-fault divorce.)

The Heritage Foundation's Fagan goes even further:

> The root cause of poverty and income disparity is linked undeniably to the presence or absence of marriage." In 1950, 12 percent of children entered a broken family some time before their nineteenth birthday; in 1992 the comparable figure was 58 percent. Children living with a single mother are six times as likely to be in poverty as children living with married parents. And 73 percent of the poorest 20 percent of American families are single-parent households; 95 percent of the wealthiest 20 percent are headed by married couples.

Cohabitation doubles the rate of divorce; cohabitation with someone other than the eventual spouse quadruples the rate. Single-parent children or step children are three times more likely to drop out of school.

WHAT ARE THE WORST FINANCIAL AND
EMOTIONAL CONSEQUENCES OF DIVORCE?

People from every political stripe and every religious background see the terrific cost of careless marriage and the trouble it brings in its wake.

Scott M. Stanley and Howard J. Markman, of the University of Denver and PREP, Inc., have written, "The 'triple threat' of marital conflict, divorce, and out-of-wedlock births has led to a generation of U. S. children at great risk for poverty, health problems, alienation, and antisocial behavior."

Chuck Colson, former special counsel to President Nixon, convicted Watergate figure, founder of Prison Fellowship Ministries, and winner of the million-dollar Templeton Prize in religion, says, "Couples need to know that it is only when Christ is at the heart of their marriage that they will be able to resist [the] ancient pagan call" of Eros. You don't make marriage vows to Eros but to God. Loving somebody else doesn't justify breaking your vow.

A *Toronto Sun* article by Elaine Moyle focused on the relationship between the destructive effect of divorce on children and the selfish gratification their parents seek, trading the happiness and future success of their children for their own selfish ends.

Research shows that kids—once thought to be resilient to parental separation and better off with a single, 'happy' parent—actually suffer severe emotional consequences. The phenomenon is attributed to their parents' obsession with personal gratification and belief that divorce was the instant panacea for an imperfect marriage.

While an unhappy home life creates a plethora of problems for kids, ongoing studies show divorce can create even greater emotional trauma. In fact, some experts now suggest kids are better off in mundane, hostility-free marriages than in single-parent families.

This flies in the face of all those parents and their advisors who insist a divorce is "best for the children." According to these studies, living in a household with two unhappy parents is immeasurably better for the child than living with one happy one.

How can government spending change to benefit traditional families?

Only 42 percent of children between fourteen and eighteen years old live in an intact two-parent, married family. To deal with the other 58 percent and the host of societal and public policy problems that surround them, federal and state governments spend $150 billion per year to subsidize and sustain single-parent families. They spend only a tenth that much, $150 million, to strengthen two-parent families. "Refocusing funds to preserve marriage by reducing divorce and illegitimacy not only will be good for children and society, but in the long run will save money."

Colson raises an interesting question. He writes of a minister who called in to Laura Schlessinger wondering if he should sue a couple he married who are now getting a divorce. At the rate people sue each other in this day and age, nothing would surprise me. The church does a poor job preparing couples for marriage. "The church ought to be a force for preserving the institution God has ordained as the basis of the social order."

IF I'M UNHAPPY IN MY MARRIAGE
RIGHT NOW, WHAT SHOULD I DO?

If you're unhappy in your marriage, don't get a divorce for the good of the children. Divorce is a selfish act: "I want something different; I deserve something better." A divorce won't help your children. And a divorce certainly won't trigger a fountain of heavenly blessings from God on your life.

The greatest thing you can do for your children, other than to tell them that Jesus loves them and that Jesus died for them and that Jesus has a wonderful plan for their lives, is to model before them what it means to be a biblical husband and what it means to be a biblical wife.

Don't get divorced. Work it out. Go to your local pastor; go to your local counselor; get on your knees together before God. Go back to church.

As Bill Bennett points out in *The Broken Hearth,* research has discovered that 86 percent of marriages described by the spouses as "unhappy" have become much happier and more satisfying five years later if they stayed together. In other words, as Maggie Gallagher and Linda J. Waite conclude, "permanent marital unhappiness is surprisingly rare among the couples who stick it out."

But if you are the child of divorce or an innocent party, remember that in Jesus Christ you always have hope. As the Bible assures us, God is the one who can restore the years the locusts have eaten (Joel 2:25).

CHAPTER 5

NEITHER FREE NOR LOVE

How liberated sexuality is luring us to disaster.

The number-one battle line in our country today is the struggle over sexuality. There are no gray areas here; the issues are clear and compelling. Christians, with their base in the Christian family unit, have the opportunity to reassert Judeo-Christian sexual values, and there are encouraging signs that they are doing so with greater energy and resolve than in the past. I think more and more Americans who are traditionalists at heart are beginning to see that the only alternative to getting involved in the conversation is being submerged in a polluted sea of pagan sexuality.

We live in a sex-obsessed culture. Relaxed attitudes toward human sexuality have turned the biblical notion of wholesome and monogamous sexual relations between husband and wife on its head. Many young people don't know right from wrong when it comes to their bodies—our culture tells them it's all relative. Scriptural standards of sexual purity have been abandoned. Teens and adults feel pressured by society and their peers to engage in promiscuous sexual behavior.

In the 1960s the sexual revolution exploded on the scene with breathtaking suddenness, hitting our culture with the force of a massive tidal wave, sweeping all before it. Suddenly the burden of proof switched to those who respected chastity, fidelity, monogamy, and marriage as normative and healthy in sexual relationships. And they were caught off guard; they'd never had to defend their positions before because every respectable public voice had been on their side. The sexual revolution soon became virtually synonymous with the youth counterculture, especially on college campuses. This new value system, which mocked traditional Christian concepts of chastity and even the institution of marriage itself, produced a philosophy of "free love."

As we've seen over the past three decades, this new philosophy has proven to be neither free nor love. It's not free because of the almost unimaginable cost in human suffering, wasted lives, and burdensome public expenditures. And it's certainly not love because of the unwanted and abandoned children, broken relationships, broken dreams, broken hearts, and broken bodies that promiscuous relationships inevitably produce.

It has also produced some historic presidential headlines.

WHAT DOES THE CLINTON LEGACY REVEAL ABOUT SOCIETY'S CHANGING VIEW OF SEX?

How did you explain the Clinton-Lewinsky saga to your children? First of all, the fact that you even have to explain this to them demonstrates how far we've fallen in our moral standards as a nation. Yet this is the kind of muck-wallowing behavior that's considered appropriate for the six o'clock news in our time. Immoral behavior has been with us since Old Testament days, but it's only in the past few years American news media would bring this kind of disgusting exposé into our living rooms in the mindless pursuit of ever higher ratings.

The sexual immorality of Clinton's offense, the lying, the coverup, and all the rest are folded into a society that is already up to its neck in unfettered sexuality. And the people's response shows how dangerously desensitized to this kind of behavior we've become as a society: public opinion polls reveal more concern with allegations of presidential perjury than the rumored adulterous sex acts. This is our reward for a generation of free sex and loose morals that free love begat.

If what happened in the White House were an abberational outrage, the reaction to it as a moral issue would probably have been far more pronounced. The irony is that what happened is no worse than the plot lines of popular television programs we can watch on the national networks every night of the week.

Even more alarming than President Clinton's behavior was the nation's indifference. Any middle manager or school teacher in America with such evidence against him would be fired on the spot. More than 60 percent of Americans believe some of the accusations were true; yet over 70 percent gave him a positive approval rating! This says a lot more about American society than it does about the former president. Clinton became only the second U. S. president in history to be impeached, though he was not removed from office by the Senate.

WHAT'S OUR BEST HOPE FOR RESTORING SAFE, HEALTHY MORAL CONDUCT?

The nation has lost its moral compass and is wandering aimlessly in dangerous, uncharted territory. We are a nation in pain, and there's only one cure. Only the church has the salve to heal the hurting and brokenhearted. Christian families are the keepers of the moral flame in our nation. It is our responsibility and our joy to understand and uphold the biblical model of sexuality and contend for the faith against satanic counterfeits. Americans can't imagine the heartache and hazard ahead if we don't halt this freefall into pagan sexuality.

Traditional notions have been twisted and the family revealed in Scripture has been twisted and uprooted from its biblical foundation. But the church is uniquely positioned, and in fact commanded, to sound the clarion call to a nation of people drifting deeper into a morass of immorality. If the people of God do not step forward to stand in the gap for those who are being destroyed by this poisoned pagan sexuality, we shall soon see a culture ushered to death's door. And their blood will be on our hands.

WHEN DID TRADITIONAL MORALITY LOSE ITS INFLUENCE OVER AMERICAN CULTURE?

There has been a gradual change in the way America views traditional morals—by that I mean the Judeo-Christian moral standards upon which this country was founded and which have driven its policies and laws from its earliest colonial days until about twenty years after the end of World War II. For that period of more than three hundred years, public policy reflected Judeo-Christian teaching and thinking, whether the policymakers were Christian or not. Any person or organization whose moral standards were at odds with those standards was challenged to explain itself. They were the outsiders; the burden of proof was on them.

In the sixties, everything changed, and the results by any measure have been catastrophic. Lives have been ravaged by disease, divorce, and desertion in acting out the false and destructive values of the sexual revolution. About 54 percent of high school students are sexually active (72 percent of seniors). Since 1970, unwed pregnancies are up 87 percent and abortions up 67 percent. This is the legacy of free love.

WHAT SHOULD MY RESPONSE BE TO AIDS?

Beginning in 1981, the condition that would one day be known as AIDS was first identified in America—in California, where so many trends begin. The cost of AIDS in the twenty years since is incalculable both in terms of human suffering and financial cost. Political pressure has prompted Congress to authorize many times more money per patient to treat AIDS than to treat far more common diseases and conditions such as cancer and multiple sclerosis.

While the infection rates have declined in this country, in Africa, where extramarital sexual activity is even more culturally ingrained than in the U. S. and medical facilities are few, AIDS has become a pandemic; in some countries more than a fourth of the population carries the AIDS-causing virus.

The saddest fact of all about this sad business is that AIDS is 100 percent preventable. Preservation of Christian marriage fidelity and the cecessation of intravenous drug abuse would drastically reduce the spread of AIDS overnight. And yet the government refuses to encourage marital fidelity with anywhere near the resources and sense of urgency they devote to discouraging illicit drug use.

It's like me saying I want to put my hand on a hot stove. You say, "No, you shouldn't do that, you'll hurt yourself." But instead of agreeing, I reply, "It's my privilege to put my hand on a hot stove any time I want. It's my hand. It's your job to come up with the technology to keep the stove from burning me. It's your fault." Yet that's how too many people treat AIDS. The simple fact is that the AIDS epidemic isn't a medical problem. It's a behavioral problem.

AIDS is an extreme example of the harm wrought by "free love," but there are so many more. Our children, set adrift in families ravaged by divorce and moral decay and victimized by parental neglect and abuse, are in great and mortal peril. They desperately need us to make the case for moral absolutes, especially in the area of sexuality.

WHAT IS THE GOVERNMENT DOING TO ENCOURAGE AMERICANS TO CHANGE SEXUAL BEHAVIOR THAT IS DANGEROUS, EXPENSIVE, AND EMOTIONALLY DEVASTATING?

Even in the face of all these horror stories, Americans persist in the sort of sexual behavior that causes disaster and heartbreak. Why are a third of American children born out of wedlock? According to the Population Council research report *Fertility in the United States: New Patterns, New Theories,* it's because the "opportunity cost" of childbearing and childrearing is just not sufficiently high to reduce casual pregnancy. Illegitimate births continue to rise even after hundreds of millions of dollars have been spent on sex education and birth control.

In spite of what the government knows about the financial and emotional cost of sexual promiscuity, government leaders have made it too easy for women to raise illegitimate children at government expense.

The Population Council reports "persistently high teenage childbearing and delayed childbearing by women in their 30s." America has one of the highest rates of teenage childbearing in the developed world. This is explained by low usage of contraceptives, traceable to "a social environment that romanticizes sexual activity but makes responsible sexual behavior difficult."

If you doubt that our social environment romanticizes sexual activity, I invite you to take a minute and browse at the corner newsstand or flip through the stations on your cable TV. We allow these influential sources to pound us nonstop with alluring, consequence-free sexual images, then wonder why our children, as described in a *Wall Street Journal* essay, "copulate like field animals." In 1970, 11 percent of American children were born out of wedlock; in 1992 it was 30 percent. Today it's a third. Marriage is no longer the great pivotal event in a person's life it once was, for men or women. In the post-free love era, men can pretty much find the sexual self-gratification they desire without the commitment, expense, and inconvenience of marriage.

Women do more "nonmarital childbearing" thanks to government support and the pressure of more women in the workforce. The Family Support Act of 1988 requires the establishment of paternity for all newborns and payment of child support by the biological father. So the financial downside for women is reduced. Furthermore, women with low aspirations for school or the job market don't see much of a risk in getting pregnant. What are they giving up?

The Population Council report further notes, "Any easing of the conflict between work responsibilities and childbearing will lead to an increase in fertility," and "anything that decreases the accessibility, quality, or acceptability of existing childcare arrangements, or substantially increases the cost of childcare, would likely lead to a swift decline in fertility."

ISN'T IT TRUE THAT THE VAST MAJORITY OF
UNWED PARENTS ARE TEENAGERS?

It's a common misconception that promiscuous teenagers are the major cause of out-of-wedlock births. The facts prove otherwise. Not only are most unwed mothers adults, but many unwed teenage mothers bear children fathered by adult men.

U. S. News and World Report states that "many more 20-something adults than teenagers give birth to kids out of wedlock. In fact, most of the current social ills tied to sexual behavior—not only children born to unwed parents but sexually transmitted diseases, abortions, and the like—stem chiefly from adults who have sex before they marry, not from sexually active teens."

The reporter, David Whitman, quotes statistics showing that 78 percent of unwed mothers are 19 or over, and 80 percent of women who have abortions are 20 or over.

In three-fourths of teenage pregnancies, the father is 20 or older. "Teen pregnancy is chiefly a result of these older men fathering out-of-wedlock babies with 18- and 19-year-old women, who are responsible for about three out of five teen births. Only one-fourth of males who impregnate girls under 18 are also under 18."

IS "RECREATIONAL SEX" AN ACCEPTED MAINSTREAM OPTION?

Many people believe premarital sex between consenting adults is generally positive. Richard Posner in *Sex and Reason* declares, "There is no good reason to deter premarital sex, a generally harmless source of pleasure and for some people an important stage of marital search." Some conservative libertarians don't want the government meddling in private matters, even in the defense of morality. Posner and others think if a woman can afford a child she should be able to have one, otherwise she "ought to be discouraged from having it."

Yet as we've seen, sex outside of marriage is anything but harmless.

Whitman reports, "Conservatives, quick to decry sex between unwed teens and outspoken on many other sexual issues, turn suddenly shy when asked about adult premarital liaisons. Many prominent religious figures have either come to accept such behavior or have been cowed into silence because it is too controversial within their churches. Why? Americans, at least tacitly, have all but given up on the notion that the appropriate premarital state is one of chastity." Half of Americans believe premarital sex is OK at least sometimes. And why shouldn't they? Prime-time TV gives us eight depictions of nonmarital sex for every one of married sex.

WHAT'S THE BIGGEST CASUALTY
OF THE SEXUAL REVOLUTION?

"If converting Americans to free love and loose sexual mores was the goal," Whitman continues, "the [sexual] revolution was pretty much a dud. More than 70 percent of Americans say they've only had one sexual partner in the past year; over 80 percent say they've never had an extramarital affair. Most think adultery, teenage sex, and homosexuality are 'always or almost always' wrong."

In the aftermath of the sexual revolution, "there was one definite casualty: Americans' long-held conviction that virginity should be relinquished only in the marriage bed. Almost certainly, television has had a central role in eroding the stigma of premarital sex." A *U. S. News* poll revealed 38 percent of the "Hollywood elite" worried about how TV portrayed premarital sex, while 83 percent of the public worried.

Another poll tells us that a majority of those under forty-five think adult premarital sex "generally benefits people quite apart from the issue of expanding their sexual pleasure." In other words, they think sowing your wild oats is OK. Less than half think adults should remain virgins until they marry—they think shopping around helps them find a better spouse.

But the facts tell a different—far different—and tragic story. Cohabiting couples are 33 percent more likely to divorce. They're also more likely to be involved in domestic violence, to use cocaine, and smoke cigarettes.

Has free love left Americans more sexually satisfied?

Condoning premarital sex makes it harder for authorities to curb other, more controversial types of sexual behavior—sex with minors, voluntary incest, etc. Put another way, sex before marriage has proved to be the runaway horse of traditional values.

Jennifer Grossman of MSNBC draws an important comparison between what people expected from the sexual revolution and what they got. Ironically, with unmarried sex readily available and culturally acceptable, people are "surfeited with sex and yet starved for love. This all-you-can-eat sexual buffet is leaving a lot of men and women feeling very empty. I see a pattern among my girlfriends—when they sleep with men, they cry. Sleeping with a man you've known for a week is such an 'almost.' It's almost what you want—but a chasm away from what you really need."

Who have been some high-profile defenders of traditional morals?

In 1992, Vice President Dan Quayle was roasted in the media for his pronouncement against the decision of television character Murphy Brown to have a child out of wedlock. Lisa Schiffren, the speechwriter who wrote that memorable speech, is now married and the mother of a daughter. "Among the elite," she says, "there is more public posturing about not smoking, or not being fat, than about not having promiscuous sexual relationships. People are afraid to sound like prigs. I myself have overcome this and am happy to be a prig. But I no longer have to date."

Some people get it right, and I applaud their courage and faithfulness in the face of public opposition. Bishop James McHugh of Camden, New Jersey, minces no words when he declares, "All sexual activity outside of marriage is wrong and has no moral justification." But peer pressure and the lure of media messages are strong forces to overcome. Young people who've sinned, Bishop McHugh says, "aren't so sure they want their younger brothers and sisters to live through the same experience. But they feel restrained from honestly saying what they think to upcoming generations, either from guilt, ineptitude, or fear that they will be rejected or ridiculed."

HOW CAN CHRISTIANS IMMEDIATELY AND DRAMATICALLY SLASH THE DIVORCE RATE?

Christians, it's time for a reformation. We're calling the church to a family reformation. The First Reformation came about through a return to the Word of God. The Second Reformation needs to occur around the *work* of God in the families of the churches.

How can Christians be the salt and light of the culture when the divorce rate in the church is now actually higher than that of the culture at large? The answer is, it can't. I agree whole-heartedly with Dennis Rainey, who believes we would cut divorce by 90 percent if Christians would do one thing: pray together as a couple every day. His research across the country shows that only about one in every twenty couples pray together daily.

How do we turn the tide back toward the traditional, Bible-based morality our nation's founders believed in, the morality on which they based our laws and which prompted them to choose as our national motto "In God We Trust"? PRAY! Pray with your spouse every day. If that's not possible, or if you aren't married, pray with another family member or pray by yourself. It doesn't cost anything, doesn't require legislation, has no political agenda, and puts incredible power at your fingertips.

WHAT'S THE VIEW ON FAMILIES OF AMERICA'S SOUTHERN BAPTISTS?

I am pleased to be able to say that Southern Baptists have unflinchingly endorsed the traditional family. Of course the media and the usual suspects challenged our affirmation, but the challenge is harmless—they base their view on opinion while our declaration is based on forty-two Scripture references.

Here's the statement in full, as adopted by the Southern Baptist Convention on June 9, 1998:

> God has ordained the family as the foundational institution of human society. It is composed of persons related to one another by marriage, blood, or adoption.
>
> Marriage is the uniting of one man and one woman in covenant commitment for a lifetime. It is God's unique gift to reveal the union between Christ and His church and to provide for the man and the woman in marriage the framework for intimate companionship, the channel for sexual expression according to biblical

standards, and the means for procreation of the human race.

The husband and wife are of equal worth before God, since both are created in God's image. The marriage relationship models the way God relates to His people. A husband is to love his wife as Christ loved the church. He has the God-given responsibility to provide for, to protect, and to lead his family. A wife is to submit herself graciously to the servant leadership of her husband even as the church willingly submits to the headship of Christ. She, being in the image of God as is her husband and thus equal to him, has the God-given responsibility to respect her husband and to serve as his helper in managing the household and nurturing the next generation.

Children, from the moment of conception, are a blessing and heritage from the Lord. Parents are to demonstrate to their children God's pattern for marriage. Parents are to teach their children spiritual and moral values and to lead them, through consistent lifestyle example and loving discipline, to make choices based on biblical truth. Children are to honor and obey their parents.

WHAT PROGRAM HAS HAD THE GREATEST IMPACT IN BRINGING TEENS BACK TO BIBLICAL MORALITY?

Christian standards can turn the tide. One of the best examples of this over the last ten years is the Southern Baptist True Love Waits program and its dramatic nationwide success. This wonderful ministry encourages teens to abstain from sexual relations and remain pure until their wedding.

On the night of July 29, 1994, 500,000 pledge cards from True Love Waits participants were displayed on the Mall in Washington, D.C., to cheers and kudos from the columnists and commentators. For the media to report so positively on a campaign by a conservative denomination that challenges young people to buck the overwhelming trend in today's culture was surprising but a delight. And just one more proof that God is always out there smiling on our efforts to lift Him up.

The True Love Waits pledge is: "Believing that true love waits, I make a commitment to God, myself, my family, those I date, my future mate, and my future children to be sexually pure until the day I enter a covenant marriage relationship."

Numerous school districts have asked for an adaptation of True Love Waits "without all the religious stuff." What they discover is that without the moral foundation of the religious stuff, there is no program. To their credit, the True Love Waits organization has declined to modify the curriculum.

We must never, ever underestimate the value of the divine authority of the Bible and its teaching. Therein lies our strength, day in and day out, if only we will claim it. As the apostle Paul wrote to the church in Rome, "Do not be conformed to this age, but be transformed by the renewing of your mind, so that you may discern what is the good, pleasing, and perfect will of God" (Rom. 12:2).

The Bible's model is to surrender to Jesus Christ as Lord and Savior, and to let Him transform you into what He created you and shaped you to be in your mother's womb (Ps. 139:13–16).

CHAPTER 6

WHO'S REALLY IN THE CLOSET?

SLICK PR TRANSFORMS SICK SEXUAL PERVERSION
INTO "ALTERNATIVE LIFESTYLE."

Homosexuality is particularly threatening to the family and to the American culture for two reasons. First, because it is so dangerous spiritually, emotionally, and physically. A family headed by a homosexual is the ultimate perversion of the concept of family. James Dobson has it right when he states that the homosexual agenda "is attempting to destroy the definition of marriage as being between one man and one woman. If homosexuals are successful in that effort, then marriage will lose its meaning."

The second reason homosexuality is such a threat to the family is that pro-homosexual groups are having such success in promoting the homosexual lifestyle as "normal"—nothing more than a choice like preferring jazz over rock and roll. *They're the ones who are OK, and everybody else is wrong.* Leaders of the homosexual movement don't just want to come out of the closet, they want to stuff the rest of us in there with them. Not only do they demand to be seen as normal, they demand that traditional heterosexuals be branded as society's shameful, deviant outcasts and labeled as "heterosexual supremacists."

We need to understand we're in a culture war for the hearts and minds of Americans and the hearts and minds of the next generation. And what's at stake is this bedrock issue: is homosexuality generally going to be considered a normal, healthy, acceptable lifestyle or is it to be an aberration, a sin, and deviant? Few issues in our culture today have divided us so deeply. Few are as confusing to Christians on a practical level as they consider their responses. Few threaten us as much, yet by God's grace few afford the family as much power in determining the outcome.

HOW HAS POPULAR OPINION ABOUT HOMOSEXUALITY CHANGED IN RECENT YEARS?

In these first years of the twenty-first century, we are seeing an enormous shift in the American population's opinion about homosexuality. It's not a shift that's positive to those who believe in traditional biblical morality. A 1999 Gallup Poll indicated that 50 percent of Americans thought homosexuality was an acceptable lifestyle. That's up from 34 percent in 1982. This dramatic change is not so much on account of any reinterpretation of traditional standards about same-sex relationships. Rather, it's the result of a multifaceted and extremely successful public relations campaign by homosexuals and their allies to change our minds by putting traditionalists on the defensive.

If we oppose them in any public forum, we're "bigoted" and "intolerant" and "discriminatory." Of course that's not true. But the opposition is waging a powerful case against the traditional Christian viewpoint in the media.

The homosexual lobby is making no secret of their agenda. We have the playbook of the radical homosexual community because they've shared it openly. The book is *After the Ball:*

How America Will Conquer Its Fear and Hatred of Gays in the Nineties by Marshall Kirk and Hunter Madsen. Their battle plan has been to cast homosexuals as victims, "i.e. victims of hate crimes, as oppressed minorities groaning under the yoke of heterosexist tyranny." They set out to make this a civil rights question rather than a question of morality and have had enormous success.

HOW CAN STATES PASS PRO-HOMOSEXUAL LEGISLATION EVEN WHEN MOST PEOPLE ARE AGAINST IT?

In March of 2000, the Vermont House of Representatives voted 76–69 to establish "civil unions" for homosexual couples. If that's OK, is a brother and sister "union" or a threesome next?

This kind of legislation constitutes the first blow of an ax laid to the root of any civilization, namely marriage and family. America needs to be aware of the ravenous wolves masquerading in the sheep's clothing of supposed tolerance.

Of course the media fell all over themselves reporting the state-sanctioned "liberation" of homosexuals in Vermont, but here's something the networks neglected to mention. Nine days before the House vote, fewer than 10 of Vermont's 246 communities voted in support of legal benefits for homosexual couples! The 1996 Defense of Marriage Act establishes state authority to refuse recognition of same-sex unions legal in other states. Opponents of Vermont's pending legislation generated an amendment to the state constitution upholding marriage between one man and one woman. A few radicals manipulated the state legislature against the overwhelming opposition to homosexual marriage. Many of these legislators lost their jobs in the 2000 elections as a result of the tidal wave of voter anger over their actions.

In 1993, Hawaii became the first state to rule in favor of officially sanctioned same-sex unions. Was this a response to the voice of the people of that beautiful island state? Hardly. In the fall of 1998, 69 percent of voters approved a constitutional amendment negating the 1993 court ruling in favor of homosexual marriages. Not only did more than two-thirds of Hawaiians disapprove of the law, they took action to make sure nothing like it happened again. On the same day, Alaska voters added the homosexual ban to their constitution with 68 percent of the vote.

Once you have the full story on these and other similar incidents, it's obvious that homosexual marriage is not something the country wants, regardless of how a tiny cadre of radical homosexual activists try to force it on us.

DOES THE BIBLE SPECIFICALLY CONDEMN HOMOSEXUALITY?

Homosexuals set out to neutralize the religious community, and they have done an absolutely stellar job. Many mainline Christian denominations have been torn to pieces, even to the point of possible splits among Episcopal and Methodist ranks. There are now people in positions of responsibility in these denominations, and others, who publicly insist, "Oh well, the Bible doesn't really say anything about homosexuality."

Well, that's absolute nonsense, which you know already if you've ever read the Bible. Thank God for people like John Stott and others who have made it very clear that the Bible does have a great deal to say about homosexuality in very specific and condemning words. In Romans 1 Paul specifically condemns homosexuality as a particularly abhorrent lifestyle.

He describes men and women who had their minds "darkened" (v. 21) and were delivered over by God:

> . . . in the cravings of their hearts to sexual impurity, so that their bodies were degraded among themselves. They exchanged the truth of God for a lie, and worshiped and served something created instead of the Creator, who is blessed forever. Amen.
>
> This is why God delivered them over to degrading passions. For even their females exchanged natural sexual intercourse for what is unnatural. The males in the same way also left natural sexual intercourse with females and were inflamed in their lust for one another. Males committed shameless acts with males and received in their own persons the appropriate penalty for their perversion (vv. 24–27).

Is this describing an acceptable alternative lifestyle choice? I don't think so. This happens to be the new Holman Christian Standard Bible, but you can look at any translation you want: what it says is what it says.

HOW HAS THE CHRISTIAN VIEW OF HOMOSEXUALITY BEEN WATERED DOWN?

The Christian faith for nineteen centuries—and the Jewish faith before that—had no problem understanding what God was saying about homosexuality in Scripture. All that has changed with the heterodoxy and heresy that crept into the Christian faith in the twentieth century from those who think they have the right to decide what parts of Scripture are valid and authoritative and what parts are not. They've adopted a "Dalmatian" theology: they believe the Bible is inspired in spots, and they're inspired to spot the spots. They want to stand in judgment over Scripture, and that's a dangerous place to be.

Unfortunately, even some of my Southern Baptist brethren have been misled by the homosexual lobby's powerful persuasion. A few years ago, Pullen Memorial Baptist Church in Raleigh, North Carolina, blessed a homosexual "union," and Binkley Memorial Baptist Church in the same city voted to license a homosexual divinity student. And yet, as we've seen, the Bible condemns homosexuality in unmistakable terms.

That is why the Southern Baptist Convention responded by voting overwhelmingly to amend its Constitution and Bylaws to exclude churches from the Convention that "act to affirm, approve, or endorse homosexual behavior."

It is only now, with modern liberal attitudes toward the Bible, that some would dismiss Paul's authoritative teaching as "homophobia." If we are going to be Christians under biblical authority, then we cannot accept homosexuality.

If we truly love homosexuals as Christians are called to love one another, we will no more accept their unrepentant homosexuality than we would accept an alcoholic's unrepentant drunkenness. *Agape* love does not accept sinful behavior.

Can we imagine a Southern Baptist church licensing an acknowledged, unrepentant drunkard, adulterer, or child molester to the Gospel ministry, or blessing a union of a pedophile and an underage child? What is the difference between these examples and what the two churches in North Carolina have done?

The difference is the savvy and relentless marketing of homosexuals as victims rather than as practitioners of a deviant lifestyle.

DON'T HOMOSEXUALS DESERVE TO BE TOLERATED EVEN IF WE DISAGREE WITH THEM?

If we stand under the authority of Scripture, our position will be that God loathes and detests homosexuality as a particularly unnatural lifestyle, while He loves homosexuals and lesbians and wants to deliver them out of the clutches of this destructive, abnormal, unhealthy, unnatural lifestyle—unnatural not by the standards of America, but by the standards of God Almighty. Homosexual activists have learned that being identified as an oppressed minority gives them political and socio-economic clout beyond their wildest dreams. And they are on the march everywhere.

In Connecticut not long ago, the symbol of the homosexual movement flew as a flag above the state capitol for a week. During the Clinton administration, the President of the United States allied himself with groups attempting to intervene between the beliefs of parents and the teaching of their children by having so-called "tolerance education" in middle schools.

Now what does "tolerance education" mean? Tolerance can be a good thing or a bad thing, depending on the application. In the hands of the foes of biblical authority, tolerance education meant that it was vicious and ugly and evil and hateful and primitive and backward to say that homosexuality was immoral and that homosexuality was sin. Why then don't we tolerate polygamy, sex with children, or incest? Those are all just lifestyles—how can we impose our subjective morality on them? The difference is that polygamists and pedophiles and the incestuous don't have the public relations savvy the homosexual movement in America possesses.

CAN CONDEMNATION OF HOMOSEXUALS
ACTUALLY PROMOTE THEIR CAUSE?

We have to distance ourselves from one of the best friends that the homosexual movement has, Fred Phelps, pastor of Westboro Baptist Church in Topeka, Kansas (which, by the way is not affiliated with the Southern Baptist Convention). People like Phelps who go around with signs that say "God hates fags" are unwittingly one of the best weapons of the homosexual movement.

We're in the business of redemption, not retribution, and that's why I am convinced that, unwittingly, Fred Phelps is doing far more to promote homosexuality than he is to discourage it. What Phelps forgets is that there were converted homosexuals in Corinth who through the saving Gospel of Jesus Christ had been forgiven and made whole (see 1 Cor. 6:9–11).

Phelps insists "fag" is "a Bible word" and that the Southern Baptists have continued to perpetuate "this soul-damning lie that God loves everybody." To me his position is a blasphemous contradiction of Christ's message of redeeming love as supremely revealed in the person and sacrificial death of Jesus Christ. These twisted, sub-biblical perversions of the Christian faith are particularly dangerous in an increasingly biblically illiterate society. I hope you will join me in continuing to pray for Phelps and his followers and hope he is spared a continuing career as an unwitting pawn and tool of the homosexual lobby.

Most Christians don't agree with Phelps, though he gets much attention on the news nationally. As Christians, we need to make it clear to anyone who will listen that we reject and refute his stance. God does not hate homosexuals. God hates homosexuality. And God wants to redeem them from that lifestyle.

Is AIDS a message from God about sexual purity?

The HIV virus and AIDS are tragic, brutal killers; men and women afflicted with them need our love and concern, our prayers and our compassion. We need to express love and concern for people with AIDS. There's no better way to demonstrate the love of Jesus than to be involved in seeking to minister to AIDS patients, to care for them and touch them—the lepers of the twenty-first century. Condemning these people is not the Christian way.

In America, a high percentage of AIDS cases are the result of sex outside marriage, the bitter fruit of sex in violation of biblical mandates. Whether it leads to AIDS or not, sex outside the emotional bond of mutual respect and responsibility only marriage can provide is a one-way ticket to disaster. The apostle Paul tells us there is no such thing as casual sex. Sexual sin is the worst kind of sin because you become part of everyone with whom you engage in sexual activity (see 1 Cor. 6:15–20). AIDS victims are a call to service, but the disease is also a warning for those who would disobey God's mandate for human sexuality.

What's wrong with homosexuals in the military?

The homosexual agenda has gone beyond the point of insisting the homosexual life is a normal life and have declared homosexuals should serve in the military. For years President Clinton pursued a policy dictated by the homosexual political lobby and opposed by the overwhelming majority of military personnel to insist that homosexual soldiers be treated like everyone else. I'm deeply concerned for our nation when the president will use the power of his office to extol and defend such reprehensible, immoral behavior.

And, just for a moment, forget how reprehensible homosexuality is in God's eyes and consider the practical aspects of homosexuals in the military. When men and women are training in dangerous, exhausting conditions, when they are deployed in the field, each person responsible for the lives of the others, is this the time for them to be worrying about being propositioned by a homosexual? To worry about their physical safety living in close quarters with deviants? To be distracted by physical relationships and jealousies when they're supposed to be defending the country?

How can military discipline be maintained in such circumstances? How can prospective volunteers be encouraged to sign up not knowing whether or not their bunk mate might be sexually attracted to them, and if so that nothing can be done about it? And yet this is the ideal of more people in powerful and influential positions than you would dare to imagine.

God will not be mocked—that which we sow, we shall also reap. What's next—chaplains performing same-sex marriages? Should the government give same-sex couples military housing and family benefits?

When he was serving as chairman of the Joint Chiefs of Staff, Colin Powell wrote to Representative Patricia Schroeder (D.-Col.), sponsor of legislation to lift the ban on homosexuals in the military. Representative Schroeder promoted the commonly heard but entirely misleading parallel between racial discrimination and sexual discrimination.

Powell wrote, "I can assure you I need no reminders concerning the history of African-Americans in the defense of their Nation and the tribulations they faced. . . . Skin color is a benign, non-behavioral characteristic. Sexual orientation is perhaps the most profound of human behavioral characteristics. Comparison of the two is a convenient but invalid argument. I believe the privacy rights of all Americans in uniform have to be considered, especially since those rights are often infringed upon by the conditions of military service."

African-American political commentator Alan Keyes adds:

> If you say human sexual behavior is like race—not subject to choice—then it is also not subject to moral judgment. That is the ultimate goal of this entire movement . . . to destroy our ability to hold people accountable for their sexual behavior. . . . So shall we have to forgo all discrimination against all adulterers now? Against people who exploit children? Against rapists?
>
> Where do you stop in your willingness to say that human sexual behavior is a condition and not a choice? You take it back into the bedroom where it belongs . . . If you bring it out into the public arena we must fight you. I don't suggest and nobody has suggested that you punish people for homosexuality or in any way interfere with them until they step into the public arena and demand that we subvert law and institution for the sake of their indulgence.

WHAT'S THE TRUTH BEHIND THE CLAIM THAT DISNEY IS PROMOTING A PRO-HOMOSEXUAL AGENDA?

One of the saddest results of the marketing of homosexuality is the fall of the Walt Disney Company from a shining, unassailable beacon of family entertainment to a promoter of dangerous, abhorrent behavior both in the movies and in real life. Even current and former Disney employees, shocked and disappointed by recent company decisions, have said Walt Disney would be appalled at what is being promoted by the company that bears his name.

However you slice it, Disney has shifted from a pro-family to an antifamily focus in recent years. One example is that the company has hired avowed lesbian Lauren Lloyd to develop female and lesbian movies. I wonder whether *Ellen,* a much-discussed TV show on the Disney-owned American Broadcasting Company—whose title character was a lesbian who "heroically" came out of the closet—is one of the results of this initiative.

The rotten roots of Disney's pro-homosexual stance extend back almost a decade. Disney helped underwrite the 1993 Hollywood benefit for the National Gay and Lesbian Task Force. Hyperion Press, a then Disney-owned publishing subsidiary, published *Growing Up Gay,* written by three homosexuals to encourage homosexual young people, and *Separate Creation,* a book arguing that homosexuals are a third creation that should be treated as equals of males and females. Disney-owned Miramax Films produced the virulently anti-Christian movie *Priest,* and Disney-owned Hollywood Pictures produced *Chicks in White Satin,* a pro-lesbian film.

And every penny you spend at Disney World or in the Disney Store helps make it possible for Disney to underwrite such money-losing, pro-homosexual projects.

It was my privilege a few years back to appear on *60 Minutes* defending the Southern Baptist Disney boycott in an interview with Leslie Stahl. What I said then, and what I still believe today, is that Disney is pushing a Christian-bashing, family-bashing, pro-homosexual agenda. And visitors to the theme parks and classic Disney movie fans help them subsidize this destructive agenda in other venues that attacks their values and their beliefs.

I went on to say, "We're going to deny, or do the best we can to deny, the normalization of a lifestyle that we believe is abnormal, deviant, unhealthy. . . . it's not Disney-owned ABC's job to help children feel more comfortable when they have questions about their sexuality. And we're exercising our right to protest it."

Shouldn't the definition of sin change as society changes?

During the Clinton years, Vice President Al Gore remarked that God created homosexuals and is grieved at their mistreatment. God did not create homosexuals as homosexuals. Romans 1:26 tells us: "God delivered them over to degrading passions." That means God created them as human beings and eventually gave them over to *their* vile passions. As is often the case, God is being blamed here for something he had nothing to do with.

Former Vice President Gore's comment was a slick effort to change the question under consideration. The debate has never been about persecution and discrimination, but rather about whether as a society we are going to normalize deviant and abhorrent sexual behavior and at the same time stigmatize those who follow the Bible in condemning such behavior.

There are those who want to redefine the sin of homosexuality out of existence. If only we could rid the world of sin so easily. But we can't. Homosexuals and lesbians are products of a sinful heart—individual as well as societal—in the form of absent fathers, childhood sexual abuse, and personal choices to engage in behavior God has condemned as both wrong and unnatural.

The church has fallen down mightily in its responsibility to speak out on this issue. For example, President Clinton issued a presidential proclamation for Gay and Lesbian Pride Month. President Clinton is a member of a Southern Baptist church. I agreed with then-president of the SBC Paige Patterson when he called for Clinton's church to exercise church discipline over him for taking a position "in outright contradistinction to the Word of God." Clinton's pastor declined to comment.

This presidential proclamation said in part that Americans were to observe the month "with appropriate programs, ceremonies and activities that celebrate our diversity. . . ."

SHOULD HOMOSEXUALS BE BOY SCOUT LEADERS?

Nothing demonstrates the political power of the homosexuals more vividly than the lawsuit they won in New Jersey in 1991 against the Boy Scouts of America challenging the Scouts' ban on homosexual leaders. The Scouts appealed to the Supreme Court, where their attorney argued, "The decision to require Boy Scouts of America, perhaps this nation's premiere private youth organization, to appoint leaders who do not accept the organization's moral code is an unprecedented intrusion into the autonomy of private organizations, throwing aside constitutional principles of free speech and association," and that homosexual activity violates the Scout Oath and Law.

"It is not the business of governments or hostile litigants to decide what a private organization's message is," the argument continued. "The Oath and Law belong to Scouting, and Scouting has the sole right to interpret them. . . . Scouting is entitled to shape its own message, and if it believes that an individual who seeks to be a uniformed Scout leader will not represent that message, it is entitled to decline his offer to volunteer services."

The Ethics & Religious Liberty Commission of the Southern Baptist Convention, which I serve as president, filed a friend of the court brief in support of the Boy Scouts. Our position was that private organizations with a moral viewpoint must retain the right to select their own leaders. If a government entity is allowed to impose on such organizations who may or may not be their leaders, what will stop them from doing the same to religious organizations next, and then local churches?

Now here's the kicker: If this case hadn't involved homosexuality—if it had involved child molesters or drug users or alcoholics—it would have been a slam-dunk for the Boy Scouts. But because homosexuality has become such a political hot potato, the standards were different.

Eventually the Supreme Court overturned the New Jersey ruling and affirmed the Boy Scouts' right to exclude homosexuals. On one hand, this has cost the Scouts financially, not only in legal fees, but in the withdrawal of financial support from organizations that now consider the Scouts "discriminatory" (even though their policy on homosexuals now is the same as it was ten years ago, even fifty years ago). But on the other hand, the Supreme Court ruling established the right of morally upright organizations to refuse admission to those whose moral standards are different.

Imagine for a moment the devastating impact on scouting if homosexual leaders were allowed. A homosexual by definition is sexually attracted to men and boys in the same way a heterosexual man is attracted to women and girls. What parent or organization in their right mind would condone heterosexual male Girl Scout leaders going on camp-outs with Girl Scouts? Even non-Christians ought to see the everyday common sense in the Boy Scouts' position on this issue. But, alas, many of them obviously don't.

DO ALL CHRISTIANS OPPOSE HOMOSEXUALITY?

Various public pronouncements cloud the Christian position on homosexuality, such as the declaration issued by the Sexuality Information and Education Council of the United States calling for the full inclusion of women and sexual minorities in congregational life, including their ordination, and the blessing of same-sex unions; also for a religious commitment to sexual and reproductive rights including abortion, and lifelong age-appropriate sexuality education. Instead of relying on the Bible, this declaration calls for "theological reflection that integrates the wisdom of excluded, often silenced peoples, and insights about sexuality from medicine, social science, the arts and the humanities."

To the extent that its sub-biblical, pagan sexual mores are endorsed by those claiming to speak from a Judeo-Christian tradition, this type of statement illustrates the significant apostasy of many within formerly Christian traditions which have made such paganization possible. Christians should follow the Bible's teaching on sexuality, which is clear, forthright, and substantial. There's no guesswork involved as long as you can read.

This is an issue that won't go away. You can't repress sexuality, and you can't ignore the parameters and limits around sex established by God. God created us as sexual beings, and he intends for us to express our sexuality within the confines of a lifelong covenant marriage relationship between one man and one woman, in which we are designed by Him to experience an intimacy and a knowing and being known that is beyond all other human relationships.

Yet are we as Christians united on the defense of this "sacred institution"? Hardly. The Illinois United Methodist Conference has criticized the Southern Baptist Convention for its stance on homosexuality, calling it "rigidly doctrinal" and "legalistic about people's lives."

I take that as a compliment, because it shows we are being obedient and faithful in practice concerning God's standard for living. True love is tough love. Tough love tells the truth. The truth revealed in Scripture is that homosexual behavior is an abomination to God and that in the love and power of Christ, homosexuals and lesbians can be delivered from this lifestyle as were some of the church members in Corinth (1 Cor. 6:9–11): "Do you not know that the unjust will not inherit God's kingdom? Do not be deceived: no sexually immoral people, idolaters, adulterers, male prostitutes, homosexuals . . . will inherit God's kingdom. Some of you were like this; but you were washed, you were sanctified, you were justified in the name of the Lord Jesus Christ and by the Spirit of our God."

The New American Standard Bible says no "boy prostitutes nor practicing homosexuals." The Greek original condemns first the passive effeminate male and then the aggressive masculine male in homosexual encounters.

Thankfully, at least at present, the majority of Methodists are holding fast to their denomination's "strong and uncompromising stance" against homosexuality.

Is tolerance the ultimate goal of homosexual activists?

Andrea Gomez, a former lesbian activist who now heads *Stop the Cycle*, thinks what the argument comes down to is "where we stand with Jesus Christ. The controversy is being played out on the field of homosexuality, but it is really about the authority of the Bible."

Unfortunately though, in today's litigious society there's a defense for just about everything. The Kentucky Baptist Homes for Children fired a lesbian employee after she came out of the closet by entering a photo of herself (wearing an "Isle of Lesbos" T-shirt) and her lover in a contest at the Kentucky State Fair. It is astounding and profoundly disturbing that Americans United for Separation of Church and State and the ACLU, both of whom came running to her defense, would argue that a children's home deciding not to have a lesbian family specialist in direct contact with children was advancing the Christian faith.

There was a time in the not-too-distant past when such actions would be described as common sense and basic decency. The argument on its face is preposterous; however, it does show the inherent danger of government meddling when faith-based institutions accept government money, even to do charitable work such as providing children's homes. Homosexuals are not good role models for children, many of whom have been sexually abused prior to arriving at the children's home.

Homosexuals don't want tolerance; that's what they have. What they really demand is acceptance of their lifestyle, protection for their sexual practices, and demonization of any who dare oppose them. Biblically faithful Christians will continue to demand the opposite. In the Kentucky case, those opposing the children's home argued that children who might have sexual identity problems were being deprived of "positive same-sex role models," a concept that most Christians historically have found to be self-contradictory terminology.

WHAT CAN ONE PERSON OR FAMILY DO TO STOP THE NORMALIZATION OF HOMOSEXUALITY?

A Christian sexual lifestyle is a monogamous relationship between one man and one woman within the confines of holy matrimony. That means no premarital, extramarital, postmarital, homosexual, or lesbian sex. And if we don't tell our young people that, if we don't tell our children that, who will? In the face of the TV shows and provocative magazine ads and "alternative lifestyles" curriculums in middle schools, you and I have got to be diligent and tireless in our quest to keep our children on God's path.

Christians must be salt, by working for laws against immoral behavior, and light, by sharing the truth and love of Jesus in order to change a person's heart. We must speak out against homosexuality, resisting the attempts to make it an acceptable alternative lifestyle and resist attempts to provide it with the kind of civil rights protections that are afforded ethnicity and gender.

The next time you look at the world around you and think it is beyond salvation, or that there's nothing you can do, take heart. America's Christian families can do plenty. They rolled back homosexual marriage in Hawaii; they kept homosexual leaders out of the Boy Scouts; they continue to make an important impact on the Disney organization with their boycott (though Disney refuses to attribute their drop in business to a boycott, even in the face of compelling evidence).

One at a time, these thoughtful acts by concerned Christians add up. And you can be a crucial voice in halting the normalization of homosexuality. Continue to support the Boy Scouts. Encourage your boys to join a scout troop. Help find sponsors. Collect donations for them and make a contribution yourself.

Find out which members of your school board, city council, and state government oppose the homosexual agenda and support traditional family values. Write letters to them—your opinion is important to them because they'll be running for re-election one day. Let them know how you feel.

Support the Disney boycott until Disney mends its ways and returns to its traditional family values roots. If you've been considering a vacation to Disney World or Disneyland, consider an alternative, not a location where your admission fee goes to support homosexual-promoting propaganda like *Ellen* and *Growing Up Gay.*

And pray diligently for homosexuals that they might turn to Jesus for the strength and support to triumph over their sin. This is the most powerful and most important duty of all.

CHAPTER 7

DIRTY LITTLE SECRETS

The biggest star of the Information Age
is rated X.

The Internet has revolutionized communications around the world. Sadly, it has also become a digital river of slime into millions of American households. More hits on the Web are on pornographic sites than all other sites combined. This is a dirty little secret these businesses try to keep hidden as they continue resisting any kind of regulation and refuse to accept even the slightest responsibility for what they do.

Remember that lack of control isn't freedom, it's anarchy. Pornography is Satan's counterfeit of God's design. In 1 Thessalonians 4:3–5, God commands us to abstain from fornication: "For this is God's will, your sanctification: that you abstain from sexual immorality, so that each of you knows how to possess his own vessel in sanctification and honor, not with lustful desires, like the Gentiles who don't know God."

The phrase "sexual immorality" is from the Greek word *porneia,* and the English word *pornography* comes from the same word. *Porneia* refers to sexual behavior that deviates from God's moral law. Since pornography is obviously deviant sexual behavior, 1 Thessalonians 4:3–5 is telling us to abstain from it. When sin entered the world, both human beings and the environment were affected. The man and the woman who had lived together in harmony with God and who were together as one flesh and were naked and unashamed suddenly felt alienated and sought to hide themselves from God. They also discovered that the curse of sin brought the advent of a spiritual struggle between the forces of light and the forces of darkness.

Jesus tells us that we are not to engage in lust. Jesus said lust is a sin of the mind and of the will. Lust is an intense sexual desire that is preoccupied with self-gratification. It is the basis for the sin of adultery. A look of admiration can quickly degenerate into lust. It is God's will that we abstain from behavior that would feed the lust of the mind and produce sin in our lives. Unfortunately, God's will regarding lust cuts against the grain of the popular culture that feeds our sinful human appetite for immoral sexual gratification. We need God's help to control our thoughts and to control our motives.

HOW POWERFUL A MOTIVATION IS SEXUAL DESIRE?

Pornographic material is one of the most powerful weapons in the arsenal of Satan designed to undermine the moral purity of human beings. It encourages lust which then enslaves them. We know from numerous studies that sexual desire is the second most powerful motivation that human beings have, exceeded only by the survival instinct.

Pornography is a visual medium of both mental and physical images. And we must constantly remind ourselves that we live in a world that is distorted by sin and we must be careful what we think and what we see. Pornography is Satan's corruption of God's design for us as sexual beings.

The Bible tells us in 1 John 2:15–17, "Do not love the world or the things that belong to the world. If anyone loves the world, love for the Father is not in Him. Because everything that belongs to the world—the lust of the flesh, the lust of the eyes, and the pride of one's lifestyle—is not from the Father, but is from the world. And the world with its lust is passing away, but the one that does God's will remains forever."

WHAT'S THE BIBLICAL VIEW OF HUMAN SEXUALITY?

Unfortunately, one reason we have been as susceptible as a society to pornography as we have—and I think we need to frankly acknowledge this—is that far too often in the history of the American church, particularly in conservative churches, we have shied away from teaching the full biblical revelation concerning human sexuality.

We have the don'ts down. Don't do this; don't do that! Don't feel this; don't feel that! We have the 1 Corinthians 6 part down, which says our bodies are not intended for sexual immorality. But too often evangelical Christians have failed to adequately understand and adequately share with our young people the Song of Solomon. If 1 Corinthians records the "don'ts," the Song of Solomon records the "do's." The Song of Solomon tells us that God created us as sexual beings to bring us joy, pleasure, and intimacy and that two becoming one flesh is the source of the greatest intimacy that human beings can know in this life.

It's worth learning Hebrew just to learn what Adam really said when he first saw Eve. A more literal translation than the one you find in your Bibles would be something like this: "Wow! That's it!" If you think God is against sex, you need to get a good modern translation of the Song of Solomon and read it. This is the one book of Scripture that will never be the basis of the Winter Bible Study in your lifetime or mine.

God created sex. He created it to bring about the most loving, caring, giving union that a man and woman can know this side of heaven. Sex isn't dirty; sex is holy. Our culture has made it dirty by selfish misapplication.

Hebrews 13:4 tells us the marriage bed is undefiled and honorable in all. God created us as sexual beings to make of two people one person. If anyone needed to be told the appropriate place and purpose for sexual relations it was the Corinthians of the first century A.D. Corinth was the sexual cesspool of the Roman Empire. The Romans had a word for someone who had been hopelessly debauched. They'd say, "Well, Claudius has been Corinthianized." That's how bad it was in Corinth.

Corinth had retired the Olympic gold medal for sexual licentiousness and orgies in the Roman world. And it was out of the twisted, distorted, degenerate flesh market that was Corinth that the Corinthian Christians were saved. And Paul admonishes them in 1 Corinthians 6:18, "Flee from sexual immorality! 'Every sin a person can commit is outside the body,' but the person who is sexually immoral sins against his own body." Paul knew that God created us as sexual beings to make of two people one flesh, and that we cannot separate ourselves from our sexuality.

CAN'T YOU SEPARATE CASUAL SEX FROM THE SEX OF REAL COMMITMENT?

Paul says there is no such thing as casual sex. When you engage in sexual intercourse, you become part of the person with whom you engage in sexual intercourse because that's why God created sex in the first place. And so Paul is saying a person who has not engaged in sexual intercourse is a fundamentally different person than a person who has. And what's more important, a person who has been monogamous and faithful within the commitment of marriage is a fundamentally different person, having shared with and become part of one person, than someone who is promiscuous, who has engaged in sex with many people and become part of many people, who in turn have become part of them.

This flies in the face of Internet pornographers who insist that pornography is a private matter and doesn't affect anyone else. People who view pornography are changed in their view of women, their view of procreation, and their view of the world. And that means they affect you and me.

God did not create us as sexual beings merely for the purpose of procreation. He didn't look at Adam in the garden and say it's not good for man to be alone, so I'm going to give him a brood mare to give him children. He said it's not good for man to be alone, and so he made him a helpmate, a completor, and the two became one flesh. This is the means through which the human race is procreated because God wants each child to be reared in a stable environment with a mom and a dad who are committed to each other and to Him. But the reason for creating us as sexual beings was to bring about the bond, the intimacy that comes when the two become one flesh. It says that they are to leave and to cleave.

When superglue first came out, I was insufficiently respectful of all its remarkable properties. And I managed to get my thumb and finger glued together. At that moment I had an existential experience of what cleaving means, because my thumb and my finger were cleaved together. And there was no way to get the thumb and finger apart without leaving some of the thumb on the finger and some of the finger on the thumb. That is why divorce is so painful. It is an amputation of part of yourself. You become part of that one with whom you engage in intimacy and you can never "divorce" that.

God created the sexual union to establish the one flesh relationship which He says shall not be broken. We need to rediscover the understanding that in the biblical revelation of God, sex is holy. God uses the relationship between the husband and the wife to describe His relationship with Israel in the Old Testament, and Jesus' relationship with His bride, the church, in the New Testament. Sexual intimacy was created by God to bring about that intimate personal level of sharing that is beyond words.

Sometimes someone says something so well that it just seems impossible to say it better. That is how I felt when I read a letter written to Dear Abby by a "St. Louis Reader." The writer, a married woman, described how she had never enjoyed sex, even though she acknowledged that her husband was "a generous and thoughtful lover." Then, she said, "It came to me that sex . . . must be about love and giving, cherishing and adoring another person, and the other person also giving, cherishing and adoring in return—a supreme representation of unconditional love given exclusively between two people. This understanding changed everything. The next time my husband and I had sex, I thought about how much I cared about him, all the many loving things he did for me, and tried to give myself in cherishing and adoring him. It was an amazing, healing and transcendent experience unlike anything I had experienced. It was making love for the first time." I can think of no better or more moving explanation of that part of the old English marriage vows that pledge, each spouse to the other, "with my body I thee worship."

A man who was reportedly a great composer once asked Mozart if he could explain his music with words. He replied,

"Well, if I could do it with words, I wouldn't need music." The sexual union is the music that goes beyond the words in the intimate union of husband and wife. Sex was designed for the mutual pleasure of the husband and wife, as Proverbs 5:18 and 19 says: "May your fountain be blessed, and may you rejoice in the wife of your youth. As a loving doe, a graceful deer—may her breasts satisfy you always, may you ever be captivated by her love."

Isn't "lust" just another word for healthy sexual desire?

Pornography perverts and distorts all of the God-given purposes for sexual intimacy. The Internet has given that perversion more reach and power than anyone could have imagined only a few years ago. Pornography teaches people to disregard the sanctity of marriage and the one flesh concept. It teaches people to disregard the intimacy of knowing another person by encouraging sexual intercourse as a casual relationship. Sex is viewed as a form of recreation with superfcial self-gratification. Pornography also teaches self-gratification without regard for the welfare of one's sexual partner. It is narcissistic and self-centered.

Several years ago you may remember the pope was roundly criticized by this licentious civilization in which we live when he said that it was wrong and sinful for a husband to "lust" after his wife. And they said, "Well what does he know about it?" The fact is that the pope was absolutely right. A husband does not have the right to lust after his own wife. Lust and sexual desire are two entirely different things. God-given desire leads a husband to give of himself to his wife and express his love for her through sexual union. Lust seeks to objectify the other person and to use him or her as an object to gratify personal selfish desires. Pornography's understanding of sex turns God's design for sex completely on its head.

In 1992 I was honored to be one of nineteen American visitors representing the Religious Alliance Against Pornography who met with the pope to discuss solutions to the worldwide pornography crisis. There was common agreement that the problem of hard-core pornography knows and respects no national or denominational boundaries. It must be opposed by international and interfaith efforts.

The pope, a gracious host, said to us in part,

> Dear friends, your meeting is a noteworthy example of religious believers coming together in order to address one of the great social ills of our time. I am convinced that by offering the unanimous witness of our common convictions regarding the dignity of man, created by God, the followers of various religions, both now and in the future, will contribute in no small measure to the growth of that civilization of love which is founded on the principles of an authentic humanism. I encourage your worthy efforts, and I cordially invoke upon all of you the abundant blessings of Almighty God.

The pope continued,

> The family is usually the first to suffer from pornography and its damaging effects on children. Consequently, as the primary cell of society, the family must be the first champion of the battle against this evil. It is my hope that your efforts to combat the plague of pornography will help families in their delicate task of forming the consciences of the young.

WHY IS INTERNET PORN ANY WORSE THAN THE MAGAZINES AND VIDEOS AVAILABLE AT THE "ADULT" STORES IN MY TOWN?

According to the Attorney General's Commission on Pornography, rapists and sex offenders are fifteen times more likely than nonoffenders to have had exposure to hard-core pornography between six and ten years of age. One recent University of New Hampshire study clearly demonstrated a higher rape rate in states with broader availability of pornographic material. Nevada has six to seven times as many pornographic outlets as South Dakota, and it has six times the rape rate.

I hope most of you don't really have any understanding of what I'm talking about when I'm talking about hard-core pornography. It is a cancer loose in our society. As close as I want you to come to it is to read the clinical descriptions of the material in the Attorney General's report. Suffice it to say that today in the United States of America we are not talking about graphic depictions or graphic descriptions of sexual intercourse between one man and one woman. That makes up less than 10 percent of the hard-core pornography that is sold in the United States. The rest includes group sex, homosexual sex, lesbian sex, bestiality, sex between adults and children, torture, rape, and sadomasochism. And with that great communications miracle, the Internet, material that was once available only in the worst back alleys of the worst cities of America is now available to anyone anywhere in the country with a computer and a modem.

I'm talking about cyber-sex, cyber-porn, grotesque obscenity which is accessible across the length and breadth of our land through the various on-line computer networks reaching into ever-increasing millions of our homes each year. I'm talking about a subterranean electronic river of slime that is pure, undistilled evil. Cyber-porn's increasing presence in our society generated cover stories in *Newsweek* and *Time* in the same week as far back as 1995. Even a cursory study of the material available on the Internet reveals what *Newsweek* accurately called "a plethora of cyber-sleaze." This material is vile, obscene, and perverse. It includes graphic depictions of bestiality, incest, pedophilia, necrophilia, defecation, urination, and torture, bondage, and rapes of women and children including bound women being burned by cigarettes and pierced with swords.

Cyber-porn on the Internet—the muck unearthed by more than half of all Web site hits in America every day—is far more deviant, violent, and perverse than what is available in the worst X-rated video or book store in most American cities.

For many men and boys, pornographic material is highly addictive. And exposure to it, particularly with the easy access of the Internet, often leads to socially destructive behavior for both themselves and their victims. Cyber-porn allows an invisible horde of pedophiles and child molesters to surf the Internet, seeking to solicit and seduce children through computer terminals often in the children's own bedrooms or homes. And yet when we managed to get a law passed through the Congress of the United States that would restrict hard-core pornography in cyberspace over the opposition of some prominent Republicans as well as Democrats, the Supreme Court struck it down.

In doing so the Supreme Court said, in this increasingly antichild society that kills about 1.2 million babies a year before they're even born, an adult's right to see anything he wants on the Internet takes precedence over this society's obligation and right to protect its minor children from exposure to this radioactive filth. That Supreme Court decision shows the depth to which we have sunk in the adult narcissism of our antichild culture.

Isn't the "Playboy lifestyle" merely a harmless fantasy?

Think about the hundreds of thousands of boys and men whose lives have been stunted and shriveled and shrunk by their exposure to hard-core pornography in their formative years. Many of them become addicted. And for every one that goes on to become a rapist and a pedophile there are tens of thousands who have had their ability to be the husbands and fathers that God intended them to be destroyed by this filth.

Now, I want to quote from the Attorney General's report. One woman testified before the committee that the incest in her life started at the age of eight. "I did not understand any of it, and I did not feel that it was right. My dad would try to convince me it was OK. He would find magazines with articles and/or pictures that would show fathers and daughters. He would say that if it was published in magazines, it had to be all right because magazines could not publish lies."

I had a prosecutor tell me that he asked child molesters, "What is the one thing I can do to keep you from doing what you're doing?" And they invariably said, "Take away our pornography." Because they use the pornography to seduce and entice and then blackmail small children.

There was also in the commission's report testimony from a woman who had been a Playboy Bunny in Hugh Hefner's *Playboy* magazine. And here's what she said: "As a little girl I found *Playboy* around the house." (Seventy-five percent of pornography is seen by children. I don't care where parents hide it; kids will find it.)

The former Playboy Bunny testified:

> What a distorted image of sexuality this gave me.
> Pornography portrays sex as impersonal and insatiable.
> It depicts everything from orgies to sadism to incest to
> bestiality. I never questioned the morality of becoming
> a Playboy Bunny because the magazine was accepted at
> home. I found that premarital sex with single men led
> me to affairs with married men. I looked on men as
> power objects. . . . in the attempt to become a movie
> star. I experienced everything from date rape to physi-
> cal abuse to group sex, and finally to fantasizing homo-
> sexuality as I read *Playboy* magazine.
>
> The Playboy philosophy gave me no warning as to
> the emotional, physical, and spiritual devastation that
> accompanied supposed sexual liberation. In reality it
> was an addiction to sexual perversion. I was extremely
> suicidal, and I sought psychiatric help for the eight
> years I lived in a promiscuous fashion.

After her conversion to Christ, this former Playboy Bunny abstained from sex until her marriage three years later where she said she has found beauty, joy, fulfillment, and peace of sex within a loving marriage. And she is no longer depressed or suicidal. "I ask you to judge," she said of the commission, "which philosophy gives freedom—Hefner's or Christ's."

As ruinous as it is, *Playboy* is decidedly soft-core porno-graphy compared to much of what is readily available in America today. Soft-core porn though will almost always pave the way for a demand to acquire ever more hard-core materials.

IS ADDICTION TO PORNOGRAPHY SOMETHING PEOPLE ARE BORN WITH?

Most evidence suggests that *all* sexual deviations and their variations are learned behavior and pornography and pornographers are the teachers. Victor Klein, professor of psychology at the University of Utah, testified to the devastating results of pornography in his statement before the Attorney General's Commission: "Vivid sexual memories and fantasies are masturbated to which at the moment of climax further reinforces their linkage to the brain and leads in time to increased probability of their being acted out in real life behavior."

Put more simply, a certain percentage of adolescents whose first sexual experiences are triggered by pornography or violent sex will develop a fetish, a conditioning that they will associate sex with violence. We are training rapists, molesters and murderers with pornography. "Pornography's the theory," Dr. James Dobson pointed out to the commission. "Rape is the practice."

Pornography is everywhere. And it creates a greater need, an ever greater hit, an ever more spectacular fix. Pornography is a whole lot worse than it was twenty years ago in America, and the reason is the old stuff no longer gives the same kick. There's a direct causal relationship between the epidemic of pornography that is engulfing us and the fact that federal authorities tell us now that a six-year-old American girl has a one-in-three chance of being sexually molested before her sixteenth birthday and a six-year-old American boy has between a one-in-five and a one-in-seven chance of being sexually molested by his sixteenth birthday.

HOW PERVASIVE IS PORNOGRAPHY IN AMERICA TODAY?

My wife is a marriage and family therapist by profession, and she and her colleagues will tell you that pornography is the great hidden cause of divorce in America today. How pervasive is it? According to *U.S. News & World Report,* "Pornography is an 8.5 to 10 billion dollar-a-year industry." Let me put that into perspective for you. We spent 6 billion dollars last year on movie tickets in America. We spent 5.5 billion on records, CDs, and cassette tapes of popular music. We spent 8.5 to 10 billion on hard-core pornography. And since 99 percent of that pornography is consumed by males, who make up 47 percent of the population, you figure out how pervasive it is.

There have been surveys done that show 100-percent exposure to hard-core pornography by eighteen-year-old American boys who are graduating from high school. A godly Christian mother shared the story with me a few years ago about her son who went off the tracks, and they could never figure out what went wrong with him. Finally, after he grew up, got married, and divorced his wife, the problem was revealed. This woman's daughter-in-law said, "Your son is a porn addict."

His addiction could be traced back to some porn magazines he and some other boys found abandoned shortly after his eleventh birthday. Her son brought them home and hid them behind the drawer in his desk. And this woman who was now weeping said to me, "Dr. Land, it was just when he was about eleven-and-a-half that we began to lose him."

We began to lose him. It's like leaving radioactive waste around for our children to find and be fatally contaminated. If being the salt of the earth means anything, it means burning this cancer out of our nation. And it will not happen unless we insist that it happens. Oh, they'll call us blue-nosers, they'll call us prudes, but the future of our children and our grandchildren and the future of our nation is at stake. We've got to be the salt of the earth, and if it burns, if it stings, if it irritates, so be it.

Promise Keepers says 62 percent of the men who attended their rallies over the past two years—and let's understand these are the good guys, the guys who want to be good husbands and fathers, who want to shoulder their responsibilities and be men instead of losers—62 percent of them acknowledged in surveys they had significant, serious problems with sexual sin and pornography. Pornography's in your church. Pornography's in your family. Pornography's on your street. It may be in your home. You must let Christ use you as the moral disinfectant salt He called you and me to be in order to stop this plague. Or it will engulf us, paganize us, and brutalize us. Eventually, we will not even recognize our own country after it has been ravaged by the catastrophic impact of rampant pornography.

We are being inundated with a tidal wave of moral relativism which centers on human sexuality. In 1960, hard-core pornography was a five to ten-million-dollar-a-year industry in America. Today, it is an eight-and-a-half to ten-billion-dollar-a-year industry. In the United States by 1996, there were more hard-core pornography outlets than there were McDonald's restaurants. Pornography is the third-largest source of revenue for organized crime in the United States, exceeded only by illegal drugs and gambling.

Still, some people wonder what all the fuss is about. They should consider that in America a woman is raped every forty-six seconds. And every nine seconds a woman is being physically beaten by either her husband or her domestic partner.

There are two dozen sexually transmitted diseases in the United States that are officially at epidemic stage. There are twelve million new cases of sexually transmitted disease (STD) in the U.S. every year and three million of those are teenagers.

WHY IS IT SO DIFFICULT FOR PORNOGRAPHY ADDICTS TO ASK FOR HELP?

Henry Rogers, a gifted author, speaker, and company chaplain for Interstate Batteries, was a guest on my radio program, *For Faith & Family*. In sharing his testimony he confessed his past addiction to pornography and talked about the difficulty men have seeking help for this condition:

> I can go into any church in Dallas on Sunday and stand up in front of the whole congregation and say, "Will ya'll pray for me because I'm struggling with greed? And it's sin and I'm ashamed of it." But I'm not going to stand in front of anybody and tell them I've got a problem with pornography, because I'm convinced you're going to judge me, you're going to condemn me. And if you go into adult bookstores you'll find that these aren't places where a lot of talking's going on. So I think even for non-believers they know this is not a place where they need to be.

He had strong words for anyone who sees pornography as a "private matter" that "doesn't hurt anybody": "The whole pornography industry is surrounded and engulfed in deception, and that's one of them as well. We will believe that this is a victimless crime, and that I'm not hurting my wife or my children or my relationship with God. And yet nothing is further from the truth."

In his book *The Silent War,* Rogers argues that pornography is not an issue of free speech, it's an issue of decency. As he continued in his interview:

> That's one of the things that just makes me crazy. In fact, I think if our founding fathers could see what we were doing with free speech, they would just shudder. It is about decency. I mean, if we want to carry that argument to the extreme then why can't we have hard-core porn movies on prime time?
>
> But it is about decency. And it is about protecting our children and being concerned about the next generation.

Pornography is truly spiritual and emotional toxic waste. And the younger you are when you're exposed to it, the more damaging it is. It's just like as adults we would not be damaged by exposure to toxic waste in the way that our children would be because we have fully developed nervous systems and fully developed bodies so we're not as vulnerable. The same thing's true with pornography: the impact on a twelve-year-old boy is going to be far more instantaneously damaging than it would be to a forty-year-old man.

As Rogers points out, "We're quick to filter the water in our homes because we're concerned about the impurities. But we need to filter the impurities that can enter into the eye-gate as well and be concerned about that."

As we said earlier in reference to television, the argument that this material doesn't have an impact on you is absolutely indefensible. If it doesn't really impact anybody, why do people spend enormous amounts of money advertising and providing Internet porn? Because it does have an impact. It has an incredible impact. The whole entertainment industry is built on that impact.

HOW CAN I PROTECT MY FAMILY
FROM INTERNET SLEAZE?

We are weak, fallible creatures and subject to temptation. Adrian Rogers offers sage advice when he says, "To avoid falling down, don't walk on slippery surfaces." That sounds so simple, but it can prevent so much tragedy and heartbreak. Steer clear of temptation and see that your family does the same. Don't pick up that magazine or click that mouse if you suspect it will subject you to temptation you know you ought to stay away from.

If you have the Internet in your house, make sure you have a reliable filter that screens out the so-called "adult" sites. If you are unfamiliar with such filters, contact a ministry you trust and they can guide you to one of the excellent products available. You need these filters, and you need to see that the computers you and members of your family use outside the home are filtered whenever possible.

Otherwise, having the Internet is like ordering a bunch of books about subjects that interest you, then having them delivered in a box mixed up with pornographic magazines you didn't order and don't want. "Well," they say, "if you want a book about baseball or American history, you have to take delivery of these others too. You don't have to look at them, though." That's what most Internet providers are telling you. I hope and pray that you'll either get a good filter or get off the Internet.

Another way you can protect your family, as well as other families, from Internet pornography is by supporting legislation to curb and control it. Whenever legislation comes up to reduce the exposure of children—and anybody else for that matter—to pornography on the Internet, support the politicians who champion it. They are fighting against long odds: the porn industry is overflowing with cash and political influence and will do all it can to keep the river of slime flowing unimpeded. Let morally responsible leaders know you're behind them. Pray for them and for yourself. And pray for the victims of pornography that they will feel the presence of God in their hearts soon, climb out of that fetid river, and bask in His glory.

CHAPTER 8

ENDANGERED SPECIES

YOU CAN KILL AN UNBORN CHILD, BUT NOT
A SNAIL-DARTER (THAT'S A FISH). GO FIGURE.

Of all the issues that face the American family today, none of them has produced more heartache or tragedy than abortion. Human life is not like any other life. The Bible tells us that God made man in His image and He breathed life into man. We are not just a part of the animal kingdom. Yet since 1973, the legal status of unborn children has been that they're not children at all, but "products of conception" that can be removed by request of the mother. How there can be a mother but no child eludes me. We have strict federal laws in the Endangered Species Act that protect the snail darter and the spotted owl. In California it's a crime to disturb a seagull's nest because the unhatched eggs represent the potential for life. And yet abortion remains legal and commonplace in this country nearly thirty years after *Roe v. Wade.*

Even so, we've reached the place now where there are endangered species of animals—snail darters and spotted owls—that have more legal protection in some states than unborn children have. You can abort your baby without penalty, but if you shoot your dog you can be arrested.

The Bible's teaching on the sanctity of each human life is unmistakable. Even so, the most endangered species in our culture is the unborn human being. At present, some turtle eggs have more legal rights than a healthy, full-term child the moment before it's born.

Sad as it seems, this news doesn't even make a ripple in the public debate any more. We've been brutalized, desensitized, and paganized by an ever-rising flood of the unborns' blood as our nation continues to abort a baby every twenty seconds. That's 3 babies a minute, 180 babies an hour, over 4,000 babies a day.

DOESN'T ABORTION ENSURE THAT EVERY CHILD BORN WILL HAVE A PURPOSE IN LIFE?

When I was in the Royal Ambassador church youth program in Houston, Texas, one of the first passages of Scripture I learned was Ephesians 2:8–10: "For by grace you are saved through faith, and this is not from yourselves; it is God's gift—not from works, so that no one can boast. For we are His making, created in Christ Jesus for good works, which God prepared ahead of time so that we should walk in them." In other words, God has a plan and a purpose for every single human life that is conceived.

Despite that biblical truth, we as Americans have aborted *one-third* of all the babies conceived in the United States since 1973. Have we aborted the next Billy Graham? He could be in the pulpit today if he had been conceived in 1973. There's a one in three chance that some mother aborted the person that God sent to find a cure for cancer. This person could now be finishing up medical school if he or she were conceived in 1974.

Have we aborted the next Dwight David Eisenhower? What about the next Douglas MacArthur or Abraham Lincoln? There is a one in three chance that we have done so. Each of those nearly forty million American babies is a child sacrifice to the pagan gods of social convention, career advancement, or material well-being.

I can still remember as a boy in Sunday school having a Bible lesson about how the people of God had become so paganized that they went down into the valley of Gehenna and there they offered up in pagan sacrifice their little children to the pagan god Molech. I could never have imagined then that I would live to see America offering up its unborn children as pagan sacrifices because they're too expensive, too embarrassing, too ill, or too inconvenient!

God help us.

WHAT DOES THE MEDICAL COMMUNITY STAND TO GAIN FROM ABORTION?

Jack Wilkie is an expert on bioethics with a gruesome story to tell about the recent discoveries of cutting up the fetuses of partial-birth abortions and using the parts and organs for research. The story really broke when a woman whose job it was to cut up the bodies came forward with her testimony of the horrors she witnessed being perpetrated on the tiny victims of partial-birth abortions.

According to Wilkie, the abortion clinic would bring this tiny little aborted child to her. This female worker then would have a stack of orders for various body organs—ten eyes, three livers, a thymus, two spleens, whatever. So she would dissect these tiny little bodies while they were still warm.

As Wilkie explains, "These late-term fetuses weren't deformed or sick or injured babies. In fact, imperfect fetuses aren't worth anything to these clinics. The people who buy these organs want normal organs. In fact some of the orders say you must test first that there's no infection like AIDS. If there's an abnormality, they don't want it. So about 90 to 95 percent of these babies are entirely normal.

"Almost as high a percentage of them could survive if merely the cord was cut, and instead of sucking out the brains they let the head be delivered. Most of these kids would be big enough to survive. They weigh between one-and-a-half and four pounds."

The little bodies were delivered to this woman whose job it was to cut out the entire liver or whatever was requested and quick-freeze it, or put it on ice or in a solution, or whatever the order specified. Then she packaged it and sent it by Federal Express to the drug researcher, government organization, or university that ordered it.

Wilkie described what happened next: "The reason this young woman came to us with this story is because the abortionist brought her a basin one day with twin girls in it and said, 'Look at the great specimens I've got for you.' Both of the little girls were alive and breathing. She said, 'Wait a minute. My contract doesn't call for this.' When she walked out of the room, the abortion doctor filled the sink with water and drowned the baby girls. Then he called her back in and said, 'OK. Now you can get to work.'"

The young woman's conscience stirred, and she reported what happened. The story grew from there to reveal a whole network of wholesalers in the business. Eyes are a hundred dollars apiece. And it's best if there's enough optic nerve attached to them. Some orders are time-specific: "Within ten minutes of fetal demise." That means that baby had to be alive within ten minutes of the time they cut the organs out. The

U. S. government orders these fetal organs for the National Institute of Health. Johns Hopkins orders them. To them these are not pieces of a human being with an immortal soul but merely medical research tissue.

This is nothing more or less than biotech cannibalism: we are literally consuming our tiniest humans in order to obtain materials for research and for the production of medicines to enhance and prolong the lives of bigger and older human beings.

I've often said there is a philosophical reason why the pro-death movement has continued to fight so hard against a law that would ban partial-birth abortions. If they ever admit that there's humanity in the fetus, if they ever acknowledge that we are dealing with human life in the womb, then they've lost the war and they know it. Then it's just a question of degrees and viability and they'll be fighting on our turf, the turf of the defense and granting of full humanity under the law to our unborn children.

But now we see another major reason why the abortion industry fought so intensely to perpetuate partial-birth abortion and to uphold the Clinton presidential veto of the Partial-Birth Abortion Bill. It's more than philosophical. This has become an extremely lucrative business. These mothers are paying large sums of money for the late-term abortions. And the abortionists are in turn getting big money for trafficking these babies' organs and body parts; the older the better, the more alive the better.

HOW DOES THE PRO-ABORTION MENTALITY AFFECT OTHER AREAS OF HEALTH CARE?

God judges us, I believe, in large part as a society, on how we deal with the most helpless and defenseless among us. We've lost our moral compass. And so there are going to be those around us—doctors, nurses, family members—who are going to give us conflicting advice, conflicting opinions. And there is no longer, as there was twenty, thirty, forty years ago, a presumption in favor of life, particularly for unborn babies.

Death has invaded the nursery and the retirement home too. We must oppose the barbaric, lethal combination of technical expertise and spiritual ignorance that would deny that there is a spirit in man that is not in the animal kingdom and would abort and experiment on the preborn, harvest fetal tissue, allow death into the nursery for our mentally and physically handicapped infants, and encourage euthanasia in hospitals and retirement homes. Unless we reverse this relentless march of death, many of the people who are aborting their children will themselves in their old age be euthanized by the very same criteria they have used to eliminate their own offspring when others consider them to be too ill, too embarrassing, too expensive, or merely too inconvenient.

WHAT'S THE HISTORICAL CHRISTIAN
PERSPECTIVE ON ABORTION?

Abortion is not about women's rights. Abortion is the only instance in our culture where we allow one human being absolute right of life and death over another human being. If Christians will not stand on this issue, on what issue will we stand? If not now, when? If not here, where? And if not you, who?

I'm against abortion because I'm a Christian. That doesn't mean pro-choice people are not Christians, or can't be Christians, but it does mean they are inconsistent.

The moral right of an unborn child to life has been defended since the earliest days of Christianity. Writing in the third century, Tertullian observed, "Murder being once and for all forbidden, we may not destroy even the child in the womb . . . To hinder a birth is merely a speedier homicide."

Thirteen centuries later the great Christian reformer John Calvin wrote, "The unborn, though enclosed in the womb of its mother, is already a human being, and it is a most monstrous crime to rob it of life . . . If it seems more horrible to kill a man in his own house than in a field, because his house is his most secure place of refuge, it ought surely to be deemed more atrocious to destroy the unborn in the womb before it has come to light."

And in the twentieth century, Dietrich Bonhoeffer eloquently affirmed that the Christian viewpoint on life in the womb was still unchanged: "Destruction of the embryo in the mother's womb is a violation of the right to live which God has bestowed upon the nascent life. To raise the question of whether we are here concerned already with a human being is merely to confuse the issue. The simple fact is that God certainly intended to create a human being and that this nascent human being has been deliberately deprived of his life . . . and that is nothing but murder."

WHAT DOES THE BIBLE SAY ABOUT ABORTION?

Every Sunday school student knows at least one of the Bible references to the sanctity of life in the womb:

> God "made me in the womb" (Job 31:15).
> ". . . knit me together in my mother's womb"
> (Ps. 139:13).
> God's "hands made me and formed me"
> (Ps. 119:73).

"... [the Lord] who formed me in the womb"
(Isa. 49:5).

"Before I formed you in the womb I knew you,
before you were born I set you apart" (Jer. 1:5).

David revealed that God had prior, pre-embryonic knowledge—comprehensive, exhaustive knowledge—of his life:

"Your eyes saw my unformed body. All the days
ordered for me were written in your book before one
of them came to be" (Ps. 139:16).

Humans are not on a level with animals, but were created
"a little lower than the heavenly beings" (Ps. 8:5) and given
dominion over the rest of creation. The difference is of kind,
not degree. We are not merely the most advanced life in the
animal kingdom, we are sacred unlike any other on earth.

Is RU-486 a legitimate alternative
to abortion?

A sly end run around the opposition to abortion in recent
years has been the abortion-inducing drug RU-486. When this
drug first came out, I went with a group of other concerned
people to Germany and France to explain to the manufactur-
ers there the opposition to it in the United States. I came away
at the time with a clear impression they understood that the
situation in the U.S. was very different from the situation in
France and that abortion was not widely accepted in this
country.

It took more than a decade, but RU-486 is with us now,
even though the U.S. didn't meet some of the guidelines the
drugmakers themselves set for introducing it into a particular
country: abortions aren't "widely accepted" and many

patients receiving it would not have satisfactory supervision. Without proper medical supervision, RU-486 will result in large numbers of deaths of women who will have complications from its use. Nonetheless, the American distributor and some voices in U. S. regulatory agencies called for unprecedented exemptions from clinical trials and medical oversight in introducing RU-486 to the American public. Even so, the overwhelming majority of doctors in America will not currently dispense the drug to their patients.

WHAT OTHER PUBLIC ISSUES IN RECENT HISTORY ARE COMPARABLE TO ABORTION?

In his foreword to *Our Southern Baptist Heritage of Life,* Timothy George warns of the "correlation between the decline in Bible-based faith and morality and the successful assault on the sanctity of human life." The trends offer a chilling parallel with the infamous genocides of Hitler. Once the German people rejected the premise that *all* human life is created by God and is sacred to him, then it became possible to do virtually anything to at least *some* human beings. The first victims of the Third Reich were not Jews but retarded German boys and girls who had *lebensunwertes Leben*—lives unworthy of life. Once we establish the idea that one life can be sacrificed for the health or convenience of another, we open the door for any life to be sacrificed.

America is practicing child sacrifice. We are sacrificing our unborn babies through abortion and our young children through abuse and neglect because we have forgotten God and worshiped and served the creature more than the Creator.

This deadly virus afflicting our society's bloodstream touches and impacts everyone. Part of the issue goes back to the question of legislating morality. Abortion laws, like every other kind, are a reflection of our moral status as a nation. Of course we can legislate morality, and we must do so if we are going to have government do the first thing God requires of it as an institution. Our forebears intended, and the Constitution of the United States provided for, a balance between morality and public virtue and a separation of the institution of the church and the institution of the state.

The First Amendment says that "Congress shall make no law respecting an establishment of religion, or prohibiting the free exercise thereof." All of the restrictions are on the government. The *government* must not establish a religion and must not interfere with the free exercise of religion. Only the government can violate the First Amendment's prohibitions, not individual Baptists or other Americans of religious faith.

To say that the First Amendment's guarantees of religious freedom and separation of church and state were somehow meant to restrict the political participation of people of faith or to disqualify their religious convictions and beliefs from consideration in the public arena of ideas is to twist and distort the First Amendment's intent and meaning beyond all recognition. Such a stance takes the single most compelling argument off the table before the debate even begins: abortion is wrong because the Bible says, repeatedly and categorically, that it's wrong.

IS ANTIABORTION LEGISLATION A MISGUIDED ATTEMPT TO LEGISLATE MORALITY?

There's nothing misguided about antiabortion legislation, but there are compelling historical precedents for it. The society and the people responsible for the First Amendment—and every other original component of our government—amply demonstrated the importance of God in the law through both word and deed. Of the revolution freeing the United States from allegiance to the English king, patriot Samuel Adams said, "We have this day restored the Sovereign to Whom all men ought to be obedient, and from the rising to the setting of the sun, let His kingdom come."

At his inauguration, George Washington proclaimed, "We ought to be no less persuaded that the propitious smiles of heaven can never be expected on a nation that disregards the eternal rules of order and right which Heaven itself has ordained." He came back to the same theme in his famous Farewell Address: "Of all the dispositions and habits which lead to political prosperity, religion and morality are indispensable supports. In vain would that man claim the tribute of patriotism who should labor to subvert these great pillars of human happiness."

Or, as John Adams said to officers of the First Brigade of Massachusetts Militia in 1798: "We have no government armed in power capable of contending in human passions unbridled by morality and religion. Our constitution was made for a moral and religious people. It is wholly inadequate for the government of any other." How prophetic those words have been.

A generation later, Daniel Webster affirmed, "Our ancestors established their system of government on morality and religious sentiment. Moral habits, they believed, cannot safely be trusted on any other foundation than religious principle, nor any government be secure which is not supported by moral habits."

There would have been no civil rights movement in America without moral laws. The same public voices that condemn religious leaders for trying to stop abortion applauded their involvement in the antiapartheid movement, civil rights, nuclear disarmament, Vietnam, and so forth. They vigorously defend free speech—unless they happen not to agree with it.

I firmly believe we should not try to legislate beliefs, but we should do everything we can to legislate behavior. There's an interesting parallel along those lines between abortion and slavery. A century and a half ago, many Americans took the position that although they would never own slaves, they couldn't impose their beliefs on slaveholders.

Of course, they were forgetting that slaveholders were imposing their beliefs on the slaves. In the same manner, people who say they would never have an abortion insist they can't interfere with another woman's right to have one, forgetting that the mother is imposing her morality on the unborn child!

We are sacrificing our children to the false gods of career and convenience. Through the wholesale slaughter of our unborn children we not only bring down God's judgment upon us for our callous disregard of human life, we also deny ourselves the great blessings God has prepared to bestow upon us and our world through our children. We are fearfully and wonderfully made. Human beings aren't born human, don't become human at some arbitrary and mysterious time; they are human beings from conception onward (Ps. 51:5).

HOW DOES ABORTION AFFECT
OTHER ETHICAL QUESTIONS?

Sanctity of human life encompasses a host of issues, among them abortion, infanticide, mercy-killing, assisted suicide, genetic engineering, and fetal tissue experimentation. Once the definition of life itself becomes relative rather than absolute, all life is at risk.

In *Dehumanizing the Vulnerable: When Word Games Take Lives,* William Brennan tells the story of Sandra Jensen, who had Downs Syndrome and an IQ of 70. She was refused a heart transplant because, the hospital told her parents, Down's Syndrome patients are not "appropriate candidates." *Lebensunwertes Leben*—lives unworthy of life.

One soldier of the Lord who never met a life unworthy of life was Mother Teresa, winner of the 1979 Nobel Peace Prize. I'll never forget the news footage of her at the National Prayer Breakfast in 1994 when she gave her heroic speech in support of the pro-life movement. With pro-abortion President Clinton on the rostrum nearby this tiny lady, almost invisible behind the lectern even though she was standing on a box, told the plain truth about abortion.

In a calm but firm tone, she said that the "greatest destroyer of peace today is abortion, because Jesus said, 'If you receive a little child, you receive me.' So every abortion is the denial of receiving Jesus, the neglect of receiving Jesus. And if we accept that a mother can kill even her own child, how can we tell other people not to kill one another? . . . Any country that accepts abortion is not teaching its people to love one another but to use any violence to get what they want."

Abortion, as awful as it is, is the thin end of the wedge, the camel's nose under the tent. We need to understand that what we are in the process of fighting is a cultural war over the definition of the nature and value of human life and whether human life is indeed distinct from other life. There are dire social consequences to America's abortion policies as well.

As a direct result of aborting nearly forty million future contributors to social security and Medicare over the last four decades, there is going to be tremendous demographic pressure in the future to ration health care to the elderly, to withhold

144 FOR FAITH & FAMILY

treatment from those who are no longer productive and working or are too weak to defend themselves from the younger in the uncivilized, barbaric jungle of the twenty-first-century United States. We see it now already with the keen interest in stem cell research. Stem cells show great promise for curing a host of illnesses. The problem is that some of those cells come from human embryos that are aborted to obtain their tissue. To harvest embryonic stem cells in order to save one life means deciding to sacrifice another life. Do we really want to be the kind of society that kills our tiniest humans for the medical benefit of older and bigger humans?

Once the issue becomes exchanging one human life for another, anything goes. What it boils down to is, if we do not put this evil genie back in the bottle we are going to end up not only with the wholesale slaughter of unborn children; we are going see a trend toward the termination of children who don't have a high predictability of productivity and success after birth. And for those in nursing homes and those in intensive care units to have the quality-of-life ethic applied to them, which means, "Are you healthy enough, are you normal enough to justify your continued existence? If not, we're going to pull the plug."

It's already happened in Holland, where it is now legal for doctors to kill sick patients at their request, or, in some circumstances, at the request of their families. As I write, Dutch legislators are pushing to lower the age of patients who can be euthanized to twelve.

How should these ethical questions be resolved?

It is wrong to kill human embryos to harvest their stem cells for research. We must protect, not harm, these young lives. We must not allow companies to trade in or to patent human cells, tissues, and organs. When atomic energy was discovered, the Atomic Energy Commission was founded to manage its development in the public interest and with public oversight. There ought to be something similar for biotechnology.

It is incumbent upon a demolition expert to make certain no one is in the building he is about to destroy. If he fails to check out the building adequately, and a homeless person or lost child is killed, it would be a very lame excuse indeed to have him claim, "I was not sure there was a person inside." Similarly, it is irresponsible for us to condone and conduct human embryo research simply because some researchers have established in their own minds an arbitrary lesser moral status for human beings in their embryonic stage of development. Human embryos are ends in themselves, not means to other ends. God has endowed these tiniest humans with "certain unalienable rights" just as he has us older humans, and among them are "life, liberty, and the pursuit of happiness."

The Bible promises us:

- Those who hope in the LORD will renew their strength. They will soar on wings like eagles; they will run and not grow weary, they will walk and not be faint (Isa. 40:31).
- For the eyes of the LORD range throughout the earth to strengthen those whose hearts are fully committed to him (2 Chron. 16:9).
- If my people, who are called by my name, will humble themselves and pray and seek my face and turn from their wicked ways, then will I hear from heaven and will forgive their sin and will heal their land (2 Chron. 7:14).

WHAT ARE THE CHANCES OF TURNING THE TIDE
AGAINST PRO-ABORTION FORCES?

The inability of the American people to summon the moral and spiritual backbone to put an end to this child sacrifice to the pagan gods of social convention, material well-being, and economic advantage is the most sobering indicator we could have of the extent of our society's corruption and paganization. Unless there is a spiritual awakening that is applied to the culture to stem this grotesque bloodshed, the next decade of our history will witness an even greater cheapening of human life in our culture.

We see, however, shimmering rays of hope. Today's pro-life movement is without precedent in American history. Never before has a grassroots movement grown to such proportions without the sponsorship and support of any of society's elites. We have succeeded in making abortion a frowned-upon procedure by most Americans, even if they are not yet prepared to make it illegal in most cases.

I still have a jarring and vivid memory of the first time I ever realized the full humanity of a human fetus. I was a sophomore in high school, and it was the day our biology class projects were due. My assigned seat was on the back row of tables in the classroom, next to a shelf where the projects were stacked.

One of my classmates, a girl whose father was an obstetrician, had prepared a project on the development of the human fetus. She had on display what I now know was a twelve-week-old human fetus. From my lab table only a few feet from the storage shelf, I could see that it was a perfectly formed little boy curled up in a glass jar filled with formaldehyde. The little baby was so undeniably human that I was deeply disturbed to see him displayed in such a casual, callous, disrespectful way.

When I finally mentioned it to my teacher, she sent me down to talk it over with the principal. When I explained my concern, his immediate response was, "Well, Richard, you're not a Catholic are you?" (Our Catholic friends should take the principal's assumption as a great compliment. They maintained the witness for the unborn when many others were uncertain or just plain wrong.)

"No, sir," I answered, surprised by his response, "I'm a Baptist, but that's terribly wrong. That's not just a science experiment, that's a human being and it should be shown proper respect."

A couple of hours later the fetus was removed from the stack of presentations and placed out of sight in a storeroom until that girl made her presentation.

From that day forward I've never seen how anyone, Christian or not, could deny a fetus was as surely a human being as you and I based on physical evidence alone. I don't see how anyone can view a picture or a film of human fetal development and dismiss those tiny children as anything less than fully human. Ever since then, I have felt a deeply personal obligation to speak for those who cannot speak for themselves.

WHAT CAN CHRISTIANS DO TO FIGHT ABORTION TODAY?

The fight for life in America is a fight every family can join. Many women who have had abortions have been abused, victimized, and abandoned by selfish men who view pregnant women as a broken sexual toy that an abortion will fix. Christians must praise and promote alternatives to abortion.

They must support mothers and babies after the child is born. Churches need to expand day-care services and job training.

Christians and churches must publicize and praise abortion alternatives such as adoption and foster care for children of mothers who don't want them. They must support ministries and programs that encourage pregnant women to keep their babies. They must volunteer for counseling, job training, day-care or child-care duties.

Other than sharing your faith in Jesus Christ with others, nothing you can do is more surely the Lord's work than saving and serving His precious children.

being is more developed and therefore in greater need in no way justifies the cannibalizing of another to benefit him.

Besides, it is not necessary to kill human embryos in order to obtain stem cells. Viable stem cells can be procured from other sources. Stem cell research is good, but killing human embryos to conduct this research or to heal human beings is neither necessary nor moral.

Ben Mitchell, associate professor of bioethics at Trinity Evangelical Divinity School, senior fellow at The Center for Bioethics and Human Dignity in suburban Chicago, and Consultant to the Southern Baptist Convention's Ethics & Religious Liberty Commission, labels stem cells from aborted embryos as "morally tainted." In fact, he predicts many conscientious citizens will refuse stem cell treatments that come from destroyed human beings. Adult stem cells from bone marrow and cells from umbilical cord blood, which can be obtained without destroying human life, have shown great promise in providing the same cures. The research focus should now be on them.

How has moral relativism affected medical research?

In a world of moral relativism, the question of fetal stem cell research boils down to a standoff between one person's opinion and another's. This results in the same paralyzing impasse in issue after issue.

RU-486 presented the same sort of ethical dilemma. The federal government approved the abortion drug RU-486, ending a controversial effort that required nearly all eight years of the Clinton administration to complete.

This was a double blow to the pro-life movement. First, and most significant, a more secretive method of killing unborn children was approved by the United States government. Second, restrictive guidelines proposed earlier by the Food and Drug Administration for the use of RU-486 were eliminated in the final version.

On human cloning, our representatives in Washington did a more morally responsible job. House Republican Conference chairman J. C. Watts, R.-Okla., declared that the bill outlawing human cloning in all its forms was "the right vehicle to stop the 'Brave New World' from invading our borders." Now that Advanced Cell Technologies of Massachusetts has announced that they have cloned a human embryo, it is even more imperative that Congress ban this dangerous and barbaric procedure.

Not long ago two competing groups announced they had finished an initial map of the human genome. President Clinton hailed the identification of nearly all of the more than three billion "letters" in the genetic blueprint as "the most important, most wondrous map ever produced by humankind." It means doctors in the future will be able to cure such diseases as Alzheimer's and cancer "by attacking their genetic roots," he said.

True, this announcement signaled the dawn of a new age in medical technology, but it also had—and has—the potential to take us on a dark sojourn into a nightmarish future. That's because all rules of responsibility have been suspended: science is being conducted in a moral dark age. The same people responsible for public policy about genetic manipulation cannot agree that unborn babies are human beings. They cannot agree that human beings and their body parts should not be owned through the patent process. They cannot agree that the disabled, infirm, and aged should be cared for in a dignified and humane manner rather than being discarded via euthanasia.

As Ben Mitchell concludes, our high-tech, results-oriented culture is "dominated by technological giants and ethical pygmies."

HAS THE PRESIDENT MADE A MORALLY RESPONSIBLE DECISION ON STEM CELL RESEARCH?

Faced with the decision whether or not to allow federal funds to be spent on embryonic stem cell research, President George W. Bush decided to federally fund embryonic stem cell research on tissue from previously aborted babies. I fear it's the first halting step toward crossing the moral barrier against killing more embryos to obtain their stem cells. These stem cells are the essential, foundational building blocks of an entire human being whose life was lost before his or her stem cells were harvested.

Having said that, I also believe the president is to be commended for a reflective, thoughtful statement in which he admirably summarized the complex issues at play in this debate and used the "bully pulpit" of the presidency to champion the humanity of human embryos. Despite enormous pressure from the media, many in the scientific community, and members of Congress, the president held the critically important line of defending the lives of our tiniest citizens for whom the life-and-death decision has not already been made. It would have been devastating to the nation and to the president had he crossed that line.

"My position on these issues is shaped by deeply held beliefs," President Bush said. "I'm a strong supporter of science and technology, and believe they have the potential for incredible good—to improve lives, to save life, to conquer disease. . . . I also believe human life is a sacred gift from our Creator. I worry about a culture that devalues life, and believe as your president I have an important obligation to foster and encourage respect for life in America and throughout the world."

The good news is that the president resisted the temptation to make his decision based on political calculation, because politically this choice is a no-win situation in that it deeply disappoints many of his fervent pro-life supporters without satisfying most of his critics. Clearly, this was a conclusion the president reached after much prayer and reflection according to the dictates of his own moral and spiritual compass.

The bad news is that I, like many pro-lifers, ultimately disagree with the decision. However, I personally believe that it is the most pro-life decision that any American president would have made facing this issue in the last half century.

How do different denominations react to the idea of stem cell research?

Martin L. Smith, chief of clinical ethics services at the University of Texas M. D. Anderson Cancer Center, said after the president's stem cell announcement, "I don't think on this issue, as in many issues, we are going to arrive at a consensus point where most people of goodwill are going to be able to agree. I think this will continue to be a dividing point." I agree.

Even Christian brothers disagree. The three largest Christian denominations in the United States—Roman Catholic, Southern Baptist, and United Methodist—have spoken against embryonic stem cell research. Pope John Paul II told Bush that embryonic stem cell research would "devalue and violate human life." Leaders of Bush's own Christian denomination, the United Methodists, sent him a letter urging him to continue an "extended moratorium on the destruction of human embryos for the purpose of stem cell or other research."

In contrast, the governing body of the Presbyterian Church (U.S.A.) has affirmed the use of embryonic tissue for research in the hope that doctors will find treatments for Parkinson's disease, Alzheimer's, diabetes, and spinal-cord injuries. Similarly, some Muslim and Jewish leaders support regulated use of embryonic stem cells and even see their use as religious and moral obligation considering the potential they have to relieve human disease and suffering.

According to an ABC News/*Washington Post* survey conducted prior to Bush's announcement, support for stem cell research varies by religious denomination.

The poll, conducted in late July 2001, said 63 percent of Americans believe the research is an important way to find cures for diseases, while 33 percent said it's wrong to use any human embryo for research.

Evangelical Protestants divided narrowly on the issue, with 46 percent supporting the research, 48 percent opposing, and 6 percent with no opinion.

Other Protestants supported stem cell research 74 percent to 22 percent. Catholics supported it by 63 percent and opposed it by 34 percent. Among those with no religious preference, 80 percent approved of the research and 16 percent were opposed.

"We would have liked him to continue the moratorium that was in place, but if you're going to do this research with federal funding, he narrowed it as much as he could," said Jay Dee Hanson of the United Methodist Board of Church and Society in Washington.

Bush had no obligation as a devout Christian to reach a different conclusion. I firmly believe he had an obligation as a Christian to do what he thought was right.

Hanson said it was naive to think Bush's spiritual concerns would completely outweigh his political ones. "I feel as president, he is obligated to take into account all of the religious traditions in this country," he said.

WHAT DO AMERICA'S CHRISTIAN LEADERS THINK OF THE PRESIDENT'S STEM CELL DECISION?

Many prominent Christian leaders were relieved by the president's action. James Dobson, whose Focus on the Family ministry speaks for many millions of American Christian families, said, "Although we grieve the loss of the babies that were sacrificed for the cells that now exist, they are now gone and those cells are there, and I think we can live with that." Dobson, an opponent of embryonic stem cell research, gave Bush's decision "generally a thumbs up."

"We were pleased by the fact that he—he may not have said it directly, he implied that life begins at conception. That's a good thing," Dobson said on CNN's *Larry King Live.*

The National Right to Life Committee was "delighted that President Bush's decision prevents the federal government from becoming a party to any further killing of human embryos for medical experimentation."

On the other hand, neither Archbishop Francis Schulte of New Orleans nor Archbishop Joseph Fiorenza of Houston, president of the U.S. Conference of Catholic Bishops, found much comfort in Bush's determination to protect existing embryos. "This decision by the president allows public money to fund research which directly destroys innocent human life," Schulte said. "This decision is morally wrong and furthers the culture of death."

"The federal government, for the first time in history, will support research that relies on the destruction of some defenseless human beings for the possible benefit to others," said Bishop Fiorenza. "However such a decision is hedged about with qualifications, it allows our nation's research enterprise to cultivate a disrespect for human life."

Ken Connor of the conservative Family Research Council compared stem cells to "the fruit of the poisonous tree" and said Bush "attempts to put a redemptive gloss on previous bad acts."

The Rev. Ronald Cole-Turner, a United Church of Christ minister and editor of *Beyond Cloning: Religion and the Remaking of Humanity*, said Bush may have found a political compromise rather than a moral one. "There's no grounds for distinguishing morally between an embryo that's destroyed yesterday and an embryo that's destroyed tomorrow," he said. "It's too much politics, not enough clear religious and philosophical commitment to an understanding of the embryo."

Once again, however, the other side sees matters differently. "Embryonic stem-cell research is illegal, immoral and unnecessary," claims Sen. Sam Brownback, R.-Kan. "If we manage the cure of some diseases and the betterment of some aspects of bodily health by means that involve the killing of the most defenseless and innocent of human beings, we will rightfully be judged harshly by history as having sought some benefits at the expense of our humanity and moral being."

WHAT HAPPENS NOW AS STEM CELL RESEARCH MOVES FORWARD?

Ben Mitchell and others see ongoing challenges as stem cell research continues. Mitchell writes:

First, the wall of separation is highly permeable. The health establishment "has tried to create a firewall between the act of destroying the embryo and the use of the stem cells in research. Tax-funded researchers will be standing with outstretched hand ready to receive the cells of destroyed embryos. The moral guilt for killing the embryo passes from one hand to the other. Whether NIH [the National Institute for Health] will admit it or not, researchers who use stem cells from destroyed embryos are morally complicit in the destruction of those embryos. After all, they are providing a market or use for those embryos.

Second, the guidelines are premature. There is growing evidence that human embryonic stem cells are not necessary for the progress of science or for potential therapies. Every day more data are released showing that other sources of stem cells hold great promise and do not require the destruction of the embryo or fetus.

Third, the NIH's argument is flawed. Human embryos, even at the earliest stages, are fully human. They would develop into fully formed infants if nurtured for nine months. We were all embryos at one time. Moreover, we have a responsibility not to harm other human beings, no matter how young.

Finally, the fact that these embryos are so-called spare embryos who would be discarded does not, therefore, entail a right for anyone to harvest their life-sustaining parts. Death-row prisoners are going to die anyway. That does not mean that we should be permitted to harvest their life-sustaining organs.

Douglas Johnson, legislative director of the National Right to Life Committee, makes a telling analogy to the whole stem cell issue: "If a law said that no federal funds may support 'research in which porpoises are destroyed' and a federal agency then told its grantees to arrange for porpoises to be caught and killed for use in federally approved experiments, everyone would recognize this as illegal."

HAS ANY OTHER DEBATE INVOLVED SUCH
POWER OF LIFE AND DEATH — TRADING ONE
LIFE FOR ANOTHER?

There's a long history of the U. S. government dealing with difficult, moral-scientific questions, the most famous surrounding decisions to build—and later use—the atomic bomb.

"In the advent of the nuclear age, there was knocking on the door of what's inside the atom," says a House aide who is closely tracking the stem cell and other biomedical issues. "There was a huge debate, and to this day, there's still a view that [the bomb] is immoral, it's wrong." But scientific advancement isn't going to stop, and sometimes the best that government can do is pick among "bad choices," he says.

Still, even if many of the breakthroughs of today are complex and pose new challenges for lawmakers, lessons can be learned from the past. Senator Bill Frist, R.-Tenn., a Harvard-trained heart surgeon, says the stem cell debate reminds him of the fight over organ transplants in the 1980s. Among other things, society at the time had to determine a definition for death, and it accepted so-called "brain death" as a viable state in which to remove an organ from one body for transplant in another.

Lawmakers then had to regulate and monitor the whole process, and important principles—such as advised consent, public openness through a national registry, and government oversight—were established that could be applied to stem cells today.

But there are limits to what history can teach, especially when it comes to the frontiers of biomedicine. Regulators are groping for ways to deal with the march of science. Some experts and commentators say Congress should get regular scientific briefings the way they do foreign policy briefings.

Sometimes the politicians get it right. The U. S. House of Representatives voted by an overwhelming majority to ban both "therapeutic cloning"—a euphemism for cloning and then killing tiny babies for research material—and the sale of treatments developed from such barbaric research conducted overseas. Let's hope and pray the Senate follows their sterling example. In these cases, the American people through their elected representatives in the House staked a claim to exercising the highest standards of moral leadership for the rest of the world when it comes to the sanctity of human life. And we can thank God for that.

WHAT SHOULD PRO-LIFERS HOPE FOR AS A NEXT STEP?

Pro-life Americans should be tremendously encouraged by the president's announcement of a presidential council on stem cell research chaired by Leon Kass, an observant Jew with a very strong record on issues respecting core human values. I hope and pray that this President's Council on Bioethics will be the first step toward a federal bioethics commission that would be modeled on the enormously successful Atomic Energy Commission, which kept America from being exposed to the dangers of Chernobyl-type reactors.

Without such a commission composed of scientific and ethics experts nominated by the president, confirmed by the Senate, and accountable to the people's elected representatives to oversee research in areas such as stem cells, cloning, and genetic engineering, we will sooner rather than later face Chernobyl-like biological catastrophes in which we will be confronted with heartrending, Frankenstein-like results of unregulated and unsupervised experimentation on human lives.

Even with such a commission in place, there's a still greater source of wisdom available to the president and to the American people: God's Holy Word.

The Bible makes it explicitly clear that a baby is a human being from conception onward. In Psalm 51, a penitent King David inspired by the Holy Spirit says, "Surely I was sinful at birth, sinful from the time my mother conceived me" (v. 5). It is clear from the original Hebrew that David is not saying there was something inherently sinful in the sexual union through which he was conceived, but that at the moment of his conception he had a sin nature. Only a human being with a soul and spirit is capable of having a sin nature, which we inherited from Adam.

Isn't it all right to harvest stem cells from spare embryos that would otherwise be wasted?

There are tens of thousands of living embryos that were conceived in attempts to help couples have babies and are cryogenically frozen in storage. Some argue that these babies are "spares" and are not going to be used by the parents, and thus are destined to either be discarded or kept in a frozen state of suspended animation. They say we might as well use them for the advancement of medical science and harvest their stem cells, killing them in the process.

The Bible tells us unequivocally that every one of those children is a human being. A courageous group of believers has started the Snowflake Embryo Adoption Program, to match up childless couples willing to adopt these embryos with parents willing to allow them to be born by the adoptive couple. The Snowflake program has already been successful in helping bring dozens of these previously frozen embryos to maturity.

Who can ever forget the adoptive father of two of these children before a congressional committee, holding these two healthy and perfectly normal toddlers in his arms and asking the congressmen, "Which one of my children do you want to sacrifice for this research?"

Sadly, the response of most natural parents of frozen embryos has been that they would be willing to donate their children to be sacrificed on the altar of scientific research, but would not allow a childless couple to bear their child and raise it as their own.

Once again the Bible speaks directly to this issue. When two women came to King Solomon, both claiming a child as their own, Solomon in his wisdom suggested the baby be killed and half given to each woman. Solomon knew the real mother would sooner give up her child than have the child die.

It says something very disturbing about our society that the instinctive mother love of even the harlot (and one of Solomon's petitioners—the real mother—was a harlot) is evidently so lacking that an overwhelming majority of these embryos' mothers would rather have them killed in the interest of science than be enabled to live normal, healthy lives as someone else's child.

In the apostle Paul's graphic description of the downward spiral of sin begetting greater sin in Romans 1, he describes how eventually, as sin works its habit on society's soul, people become "without natural affection" (v. 31 KJV), which in Greek is the word used to describe the instinctive natural love a mother has for her child.

WHO MAKES THE FINAL DECISION ON STEM CELL RESEARCH?

The final, crucial question is when it gets down to Solomon versus Frankenstein in twenty-first-century America, who wins? Who makes the decision?

You do, through the lawmakers you vote for and support. The public representatives you write, call, E-mail, and challenge at town meetings. Their power comes from you. Use it.

In the case of cloning, Solomon appears slightly ahead. In the RU-486 controversy, Frankenstein prevailed. In the complex and confusing matter of embryonic stem cell research, Solomon has a narrow lead for the present. But he can triumph only with your help.

CHAPTER 10

THE POWER TO CHANGE THE WORLD

ONE PRAYER CAN TRANSFORM
A THOUSAND HEARTS.

We've looked at quite a list of challenges to Christian families. For the past thirty-five years society's indifference and hostility to the Bible and to Christian teaching have grown at an ever-increasing pace. If you're like me, sometimes the best you can do these days is close your eyes and hold on as the winds of change whip around you and your loved ones.

But if God be for us, who can be against us? With the Lord on our side, His right will ultimately prevail. On every point where the world presses down, God's people find a way to respond.

We've seen that contemporary society scorns the biblical definition of the relationship between men and women. Yet it's the traditional families that are the happiest, healthiest, and most financially secure. Even to non-Christians, if you uphold the biblical family role models—husbands loving their wives selflessly and sacrificially like Christ loves the church, and wives submitting graciously to their husbands' leadership—you serve as a living sermon on the joy of a godly family wherever you go.

As traditional rules and relationships break down in our culture, we run the risk of collapsing into chaos. But, standing as a lighthouse to all who would see, God and His teaching call us to a life of assurance and contentment. Christian families can and must turn their backs on contemporary society's dysfunctional models along with the heartbreak and chaos they leave in their wake, and cling faithfully to God's ways and God's promises.

Everyone, including Christians, has seen the carnage wrought by the sexual revolution, the free love that was neither free nor love. A generation has been marred by perverse, self-indulgent, and irresponsible sexual liaisons, and a generation of children has grown up burdened with the baggage of a broken home. The emotional, social, and monetary cost of "free" love is in the trillions of dollars and counting. Even so, as dark as the situation might appear, there are many faithful families living for Jesus and swimming against the tide of relative morality.

The militant homosexual lobby has transformed the public debate about sexual orientation into an argument over "discrimination." They are clever, energetic, well-funded, and ruthless. And yet Hawaii has rolled back its homosexual marriage statutes, and the Boy Scouts won a Supreme Court battle to keep homosexual leaders away from vulnerable, impressionable young boys. The public at large is waking up at last to this threat to the most fundamental and indispensable building block of civilized society: the family.

Pornography is seeping into our homes through the river of Internet information we all find so convenient and informative and entertaining. It's appalling and alarming to think that many still believe this disgusting ooze should be protected by the First Amendment. Nevertheless, there are many, many good Christian leaders speaking out against Internet pornography, and many families making effective use of filters to keep out the filth, the same way a water filter keeps out pollutants.

Abortion is responsible for the killing of at least 1.2 million children every year, including the almost unimaginable horror of partial birth abortions. Abortion clinics rake in millions from preying on confused young women who are often pressured by their parents or boyfriends; then the clinics make millions more by selling the children's body parts. Out of this tragedy comes hope in the form of soldiers for the Lord like Mother Teresa and the thousands of pro-life counselors, adoption agencies, and others who continue to save lives every day.

WHAT CAN ONE PERSON DO THAT WILL MAKE ANY DIFFERENCE?

Changing anything about the way our culture works—doing something that truly makes a difference—seems overwhelming and impossible, as though nobody on earth could pull it off. Well that's right, nobody on earth can pull it off. But every Christian has the power of prayer. And through prayer, we have the power to change the world. The road is hard but far from hopeless.

You have the power of prayer at your disposal anywhere, anytime day or night. You have it right now as you read this. We're told in Scripture that the "intense prayer of the righteous is very powerful" (James 5:16). Now what does that mean? That means that our prayers are the fulcrum through which we can help change the world.

Let's look at the qualifiers here. James says that "intense prayer" is powerful. That means we pray fervently, on a regular, consistent basis, and that we pray ceaselessly. He also says this intense prayer must be offered up by a righteous person to be powerful. So the more in tune we are with God, the more obedient we are to God, the more contrite we are before God, the more powerful our prayers are going to be.

The Bible tells us exactly what to do. Listen to 2 Chronicles 7:14: "If my people, who are called by my name, will humble themselves and pray and seek my face and turn from their wicked ways, then will I hear from heaven and will forgive their sin and will heal their land." That is our part. Our part is to pray. Our part is to pray as obediently as possible, to confess sin, to appropriate forgiveness, and to trust God. Always remember, "The One who is in you is greater than the one who is in the world" (1 John 4:4); and "Who is the one who conquers the world but the one who believes that Jesus is the Son of God" (1 John 5:5).

HOW CAN WE HAVE AN IMPACT FOR CHRIST IN PUBLIC SCHOOLS WHEN CHRISTIANITY HAS BEEN BANNED FROM THE CLASSROOM?

Sometimes a person comes along who is a wonderful example of how a single individual can make a big difference for Christ in the world. I'd like to share with you a remarkable example of what can happen when one person lifts up fervent, heartfelt prayers to God.

Perhaps the most important national treasure we have is our children. God says that children are an inheritance from God. They are your inheritance. And increasingly in our post-Christian culture we see that these precious minds face challenges and negative influences that previous generations have never had to cope with, have never even imagined.

Unfortunately these pernicious influences come from the very place where parents assume their values will be upheld and supported: in our schools, sometimes from peers, sometimes from the administration and curriculum.

Since the Supreme Court outlawed state-sponsored prayer and Bible reading in public schools in the early 1960s, many people have been looking for a way to protect students' rights to express their faith while at school. The founders of our nation would be absolutely awestruck at the suggestion that anything in the Constitution prohibited or even discouraged students' freedom to discuss and share their faith with their fellow students. When students step onto public school property, they do not lose their First Amendment right to express their faith.

I've said it before and I'll say it again. If God's name uttered in a profanity is protected speech, even if it's offensive to believers, then God's name invoked in prayer is protected speech. The freedom to speak to others about religious matters is at least freedom of speech. The freedom to gather together to pray and study the Bible is at least freedom of assembly.

Between freedom of speech and freedom of assembly, our children should have an ironclad, unimpeachable right to pray according to the dictates of their own consciences in the public schools. I'm not in favor of teacher-led prayer or reading the Bible in class, but students should have the right to study their Bibles, pray, and talk about their faith during lunch, free periods, recess, or whenever the teacher declares a "limited open forum."

The teacher does this by saying, "Today we're going to talk about the environment. What do you, as students, think?" When the teacher sets the parameters of discussion like that, students have the right to say, "I believe God created the earth and he is going to hold us accountable for our stewardship of his creation." If the teacher tries to limit expression of faith as part of the discussion, the teacher has engaged in censorship of religion and violated the student's right to freedom of speech.

Religion is a very important thing in most parents' lives, and they don't want their children denied freedom of religious expression when they are required by law to be on public school property for such a large percentage of their waking hours in their formative years.

I must admit I don't expect the legal climate to change drastically any time soon. The falsehoods and half-truths flying around, coupled with the timidity on the part of too many officials and bureaucrats, make it very unlikely. However, I interviewed a guest on my radio program not long ago who is among the best examples I know of one person making a big difference for Christ in the world. And she did it with school prayer. Not prayer in the school, but, as an alternative, prayer for the school.

How did Moms In Touch get started praying for public school children?

Fern Nichols is the founder and president of Moms In Touch, an organization of moms praying for the children of America. These moms have committed to meet once a week for prayer for children in schools across the country. The movement began, as so many important movements do, with a single thought that germinated into a glorious flower in the garden of God.

It all started, Fern says, on "an unassuming day" when she was simply abiding with the Lord and pouring out her mother's heart in concern over her two oldest sons, who were just going off to junior high school. "Oh Lord," she prayed, alone in her house, "they are going to be facing things they never faced before. The peer pressure's going to be greater, girls are going to entice them. The vulgar language is going to be intense."

With no preplanning or agenda, she prayed transparently and from the heart that God would protect them and that "Satan would not have one gleeful moment of their life." It was an emotional moment for her, something she said she could "pound the table about." She humbly, faithfully prayed every mother's prayer over her boys. "Heavenly Father, You protect them, You guide them, You show them the way. Help them to keep the faith that they have."

Sitting there by herself at the kitchen table she realized these were life-changing heart issues for her and her boys. "Lord," she prayed, "I cannot bear this burden alone. I need to pray with somebody." And the Lord laid upon her heart another mom to call, a friend whom she knew had a girl going off to the same junior high. And so she called her and shared her heart about the two of them praying for their children. It wasn't going to be a time centered on visiting and fellowship; Fern had something more formal and serious in mind.

"And I said, 'This is going to be a tense hour of prayer,'" she recalled. "'There's going to be no refreshments. We're going to start and end on time. I mean, it's going to be really in prayer for our kids during that hour.' And she said, 'I'd love to come.'"

Fern developed a simple four-step program, that she and her friend tried out. After the first week they made a list of a few other moms they thought might want to join them. And that next week, as she reports, "there were maybe four or five of us for that hour. We were in warfare for our children in that school." And that was the very humble beginning of what became an international ministry.

She gives the glory to God. "I mean, people come up to me and ask, 'Fern, how did you start an international prayer ministry?' I say, 'I didn't know I was starting anything. I was just worried about my two boys.' So it started, I guess, kind of self-ishly, but God birthed it. This is His ministry."

WHAT BIBLICAL FOUNDATION IS THERE
FOR PRAYING OVER MY KIDS?

From that one meeting to share an hour of prayer between two concerned mothers, the ministry has grown to approximately 30,000 Moms In Touch groups in the United States. Every state has MIT groups, every province in Canada has them, and they're in 91 countries besides. That translates into anywhere from 100,000 to 150,000 women who are praying weekly for their children and those schools where they send them each day.

Moms In Touch receives many letters from moms who say the program has taught them how to pray, that it has changed their lives. Not only do they cover their children with prayer, they find other ways to put their newfound prayer power to work. "This has changed my relationship with my husband," writes one participant; another happily reports, "This has healed our marriage."

Fern insists:

We are just ordinary moms who come before the Lord. There's a verse in our ministry that we use as our theme verse, Lamentations 2:19: "Pour out your heart like water before the face of the Lord lifting our hands to him for the lives of our children."

So God hears the sincerity of our hearts, and as we come to him in prayer, he's teaching us how to pray. We're taking the four steps of the Moms In Touch program and using them in our quiet time. The result is that women are having quiet times like they've never had before.

Leaders who go through the program learn first and foremost to start their sessions on time. Moms are going every which way at once, and they need to know the hour is going to start on time and end on time.

WHAT DIFFERENT WAYS ARE THERE
TO PRAY FOR MY KIDS' SAFETY
AND SPIRITUAL STRENGTH?

The first segment of the hour at Moms In Touch, ten to twelve minutes, is given over to focusing on a specific attribute of God in prayer. An example might be the sovereignty of God. In that case, Fern explains, "We start at the beginning of that hour focusing on our Almighty God, and the fact that He is in charge, He is in control, He's the blessed controller of all things. And He rules with love and compassion and caring. I mean this is an incredible time when we focus on God. This is not a time when we ask for anything. This is God's time."

The second portion of the hour is silent confession. Fern and the other moms consider this an especially important time, "because if we regard iniquity in our heart, the Lord cannot hear us. And we need to go in boldly to that throne of grace, when that intercession time comes to receive mercy and help in our time of need."

Then there is a time of thanksgiving to God for answers to prayer. The women don't simply tell each other what God has done in their lives, they pray their thanksgiving aloud. That way all can share in the news of God's replies, but the words are directed heavenward. Fern says, "I mean, why would we exclude the One who answered them?"

The fourth and final part of the hour is spent making prayer requests to the Lord, not only for the children of participating moms, but for their classmates as well. They use school yearbooks to pray for the children by name. "Everything is done in prayer," Fern concludes. "We don't exclude our Father in anything."

We are involved in a spiritual struggle for the souls of our children and our nation. And I can't think of any better way to prepare for and to do battle in that war than to be on our knees in prayer for our students. Moms In Touch is a wonderful example of how God can use one person to do great things for families and for His kingdom. Because one mother made one phone call, more than 100,000 mothers around the world are covering their school children in prayer and becoming better prayer warriors in the process.

And the next big idea for faith and family could be *yours*. Don't think so? Fern Nichols didn't think so either until she allowed God to use her as His mighty warrior.

CHAPTER 11

WHERE THE HEART IS

A HAPPY HOME DEPENDS ON
THE POWER OF PRAYER.

More than a century and a half ago, Henry Ware Jr. wrote these
words:

> Happy the home when God is there,
> And love fills every breast;
> When one their wish, and one their prayer,
> And one their heavenly rest.
>
> Happy the home where prayer is heard,
> And praise is wont to rise;
> Where parents love the sacred word
> And all its wisdom prize.

Though the syntax is quaint and a little stilted to twenty-first-
century ears, I don't know that I've ever read a simpler, more
accurate expression of the relationship between a happy home
and a reliance on prayer to God. Prayer and a genuine faith in
the Creator are absolutely essential components for a con-
tented, secure family.

Mothers and fathers who would continue loving "the sacred
word" and prizing its wisdom have held fast to the Gospel in

spite of all we have seen that the culture, the media, the legal establishment, and other misguided powers of our time have done to lead them astray.

HOW HAVE MODERN SOCIAL TRENDS THREATENED THE CHRISTIAN HOME?

U.S. News & World Report has chronicled the decline in men's income relative to women's, and documented the weakened power and importance of men in the reproductive process. Where once men held most of the cards on decisions about childbearing, the decision-making ability is now more equally divided. The stigma of unwed motherhood has all but vanished, and abortion is commonplace. And so at the same time that there are more and better contraceptives than ever—and even drug-induced abortions—the numbers of single mothers and medical abortions have risen.

Widespread contraception beginning in the sixties caused this "revolutionary break" between men and women. "It put biological disputes at the center of our national life—women's rights, abortion, out-of-wedlock births, turmoil among black men and the rise of angry white men," according to *U.S. News*. After the advent of birth control pills, so the thinking went, women would be sexually liberated and still remain in control of their "reproductive rights," while men conversely would have less control over the impact of their own sexuality.

The pill should have made abortion less necessary, but women still got pregnant out of wedlock. The unanticipated consequence from past changes was that the age of "sexual liberation" liberated the man as well as the woman. Instead of marrying their pregnant partners—the old-fashioned "shotgun wedding"—the men simply ran off. After all, pregnancy wasn't their responsibility anymore. Most didn't offer child support or even split the cost of an abortion. When women didn't want or couldn't get their partners to marry them, they turned to the courts for abortion help. Women who decided not to abort suddenly flooded the culture with out-of-wedlock births.

Technology, then, generated an unexpected result: birth control caused more, not fewer, abortions and more, not fewer, illegitimate children. And more men abandoned their responsibilities.

Homes that guarantee a place of refuge and security are not only more pleasing to God, but they're healthier too. Reporting on a thirty-five-year study of Harvard male students, *USA Today* found that the healthiest study participants at fifty-five were the ones who considered their parents most caring when they were twenty. Parents are the main support anchors in a child's life; when the child feels cared for and loved it reduces the stress level, improves immune function, and produces a healthier adulthood.

WHAT'S THE FATHER'S PLACE IN TODAY'S TYPICAL HOUSEHOLD?

We've seen the importance of the presence of the father in a family in order for it to be financially, emotionally, and spiritually sound. Wade F. Horn, president of the National Fatherhood Initiative, believes the most disturbing social trend of our time is the increase in the number of children living without a father at home. In 1960, less than 10 million children lived in fatherless homes; today nearly 23 million, almost one quarter of all children, do so. "For the first time in history," Horn tells us, "the average child can expect to live some significant portion of their lives in a home without a father present."

The collapse of fatherhood has been "propelled by the twin engines of divorce and illegitimacy." The myth that children "don't need a father to develop normally" is a sad and sinister one that some public policy groups keep alive to serve their own selfish ends. (Some politically driven studies actually suggest children are better off without fathers!)

Horn's ominous picture reflects some of the same statistics we've encountered in previous chapters: Over time, physically absent fathers become psychologically absent as well. Forty percent of children in those homes have not seen their fathers in a year. More than half have never been in their father's home. By the time the child is seven-and-a-half, less than 25 percent are consistently visited by their fathers. Almost 75 percent will experience poverty before age eleven, compared with 20 percent for two-parent families.

Horn concludes, "Violent criminals are overwhelmingly male who grew up without fathers, including 60 percent of rapists, 72 percent of adolescent murderers, and 70 percent of long-term prison inmates."

Seventeen million parents need care for their kids after school. Between 2 and 8 P.M. is when 50 percent of juvenile crimes occur. More than 75 percent of first-time sexual encounters are in homes with no adults present.

WHAT'S THE RESULT OF TODAY'S TREND TOWARD ANDROGYNOUS, INTERCHANGEABLE PARENTS?

Up to the nineteenth century, the father in a family was considered responsible and liable for the character and education of his children. This began to change in America with the flowering of the Industrial Revolution, when men started going to work in the factories. Daily child-rearing decisions devolved to the mothers. The fathers gradually were transformed to the ones who brought home the paycheck.

This pattern held through the 1960s when, for the first time in American history, fathers started being defined as superfluous. Now their contributions are minimized, belittled, and degraded. We see this trend on television: from *Father Knows Best* we've morphed into shows that show fathers as sex-crazed or merely bumbling idiots.

In the past, the father's role was unique and different from the mother's. Differences were recognized as important in raising a well-adjusted and well-socialized child. The child needed both. Today's ideal parent is androgynous. According to at least one authority, "Both parents should behave so alike that their children should not be able to tell which is in the room, nor should they care."

Fathers are supposed to retrain themselves to be more like mom, spending less time with rough-and-tumble play and more time with diapers; less with encouragement and more with consolation; less with action and more with talk. In other words, be more like mom. Or just forget Dad completely and let the government take over his role through income support payments and day care.

Biblical fatherhood is the ideal, requiring fatherly love and a fatherly presence. The images of a biblical father figure are strong and powerful, capable, and protective.

WHAT ENCOURAGEMENT IS THERE FOR PEOPLE WHO THINK THE AMERICAN FAMILY IS A LOST CAUSE?

Have you ever felt like giving in and giving up as the American family seems to fall farther behind the biblical ideal? When what was once our shared public morality is derided as "judgmental" and "legalistic" or worse? Take heart from the story of Shirley and Van Hughes.

Shirley and Van are not wealthy people, not politically well-connected, not what you'd think of as intellectuals. They're just plain ordinary people with an extraordinary love for the Lord and a burden to share their faith and family with others. They're retired, with two children and four grandchildren, living in Arizona. And through a miraculous series of events, they have taken in ten other children to raise in the nurture and admonition of the Lord—ten children whose alternatives were almost certainly a life of depravation, crime, and tragedy.

I was honored to interview them on my radio show a while back. They explained they had taken in a household of ten boys and girls, all with the same mother but fathered by four different men.

When I spoke with the Hughes, the mother of these children was still a sad, unrepentant, unconverted soul, an alcoholic and gambler who left her children home alone for days at a time. She was unemployed and spent her welfare check on liquor and the gaming tables.

"The kids very seldom had any money," Shirley Hughes recalled. "Sometimes the kids would try and hide the check from her to get some food, but most of the time it was gone. One time a boyfriend of their aunt called and had the police come and pick them up."

When the police came to the house, they found that the children were terribly neglected. The baby was dehydrated and running a fever and had only a bottle of spoiled milk. Eventually, through a series of circumstances Shirley and Van opened up their hearts to the leadership of the Lord and accepted these children into their home in order to keep them together.

At first the Highes expected this to be a temporary arrangement. So, later when the welfare caseworkers asked if they
would be willing to adopt the kids, they said they wouldn't be
able to do it. "We thought we were ready for that cabin in the
woods by a lake and quiet dinners out," says Van. They had
raised their own children and were looking forward to a well-
deserved rest.

But those plans changed in March 1997 when the caseworkers said they had two families willing to adopt all ten
children between them. "That's when it hit me that they were
going to take *my* kids," Shirley exclaims. "The mother instinct
kicked in. Actually it was probably God's instinct, but it felt
like the mother instinct."

Shirley and Van talked about it and prayed about it and
decided to adopt all ten children so they could stay together.
I asked them how long it took to make such an important
decision.

"Overnight," Shirley answers. "But we prayed about it a
lot. Because you're not only looking at financial commitment,
you're looking at educational commitment. You're looking at
spiritual commitment. You're looking at the fact that 100 percent of your life now is on hold again.

"And sometimes you want to be a little bit selfish. And you
want to say, 'Hey, I did my part. My two boys know the Lord.'
But you can't go there. If God wanted us to retire in that way
then God would have taken us home, because that's where our
retirement is. But we talked about it. We weighed the pros and
cons, and we realized that most of the reasons we didn't want
to adopt were selfish.

"So we did it, and have never been more peaceful about a
decision. And we're just waiting for God's retirement now. I'm
really going to smile when I go, when God takes me. And you

look back and you've touched all of these lives, and if all them get saved, what a great feeling!"

WHAT PART SHOULD CHILDREN FROM DYSFUNCTIONAL FAMILIES HAVE IN DECIDING THEIR OWN FUTURE?

The Hughes insisted that the children themselves have a part in the decision. They hosted a pizza party and asked them to vote on whether they wanted to be adopted or not. Everybody was thrilled about the idea except for Juan, who was eight years old at the time. He asked, "What's adoption?" And when he realized it meant he would never go back to live with his birth mother, he left the table. Later Shirley found him in the hallway crying so hard that he was hyperventilating. He was grieving for his mother.

"He was the last person I would've expected to be unhappy," Shirley says. "He had been with us for two-and-a-half years when this all took place, and he was just so happy-go-lucky. He won citizenship awards. I mean, he was the one with the most sensitive heart in the house. And when he did that my heart just broke. I could do nothing but hold him.

"And when he said, 'Does this mean I'll never see my mom again?' I said, 'Juan, we don't say never here. Right now, you're mom is sick. If she should get better, then we'll all be a family together. But you know what you need to do now? You should start praying every single night that your mom gets better so that we can all be together.'

"He cried for almost two hours. The following day, however, he would not leave my side. He was afraid I was going to leave. And we thought we had resolved all of those issues. But when we did an interview for *Dateline*, all of that resurfaced, and he began crying again. And I had to leave the room. It is still so deep inside him.

"Yet this is still the same little boy who will tell you he went to garbage cans looking for food. But that mother-and-son bond will not leave, no matter what that mother does to you."

Juan's reaction is a dramatic reminder of how much impact we have as parents on our children—for good or ill. In spite of however much neglect and abuse a child endures at the hands of a parent, there's that tremendous hurt and tremendous bond that takes place and that deep desire to have a relationship.

Frank, the oldest of the ten children, had learned to do whatever it took to survive and was one of the most difficult children to reach. Van recalls that the caseworkers "had some real negative aspects in their psychological report on Frank. That he wouldn't bond. Frank was out for Frank, basically, and nobody else would matter in his life.

"He was fifteen at the time and pretty much a street-wise kid that went around kind of like a modern-day Robin Hood, stealing to feed his family. But that's not his fault. We felt that what they said in that report was unacceptable. We thought, honestly, through God, that we could touch him. And we did."

There was a time when Frank had an argument with Van. As his words became heated, Frank asked him if Van was going to hit him like the rest of his fathers did. Van just turned around and hugged him.

"He was watching what we were going to do with him," says Shirley. "He was going to push us to the limit of us throwing him out. And when he reached that limit and he knew he was on his last leg, he started getting trust enough and started turning himself around."

"I felt in the beginning that Frank wasn't going to make it," Van responds. "But you know what? A little love goes a long way."

WHAT PART DOES FAITH HAVE IN
REACHING OUT TO BROKEN FAMILIES?

Frank's story is a critical reminder that what's in a psychological report and what the experts say must always be weighed against the miraculous power of prayer. You can't quantify God; you can't put what God is able to do in a test tube. As Van advises, "You can look at all the books in the world and you can look at all the parenting books, but if you don't look at the Bible, you're not going to make it."

Shirley and Van had no interest in celebrity or blowing their own horn. The reason they agreed to appear on *For Faith & Family,* as well as *Dateline* and all the rest, was to publicize and promote adoption, especially of older children. "There are so many children just sitting there waiting," Shirley points out. "And I realize that a lot of people that want to adopt want babies. But what do you say to a twelve-year-old or a fourteen-year-old that has no one? What greater gift can you give a child than to give them a born-again life? And only Christians can do that."

"Only Christians can bring them who Jesus is. And God didn't leave us here just to meander around and do what we want and see him on Sunday mornings. God gave us a commission for every day, twenty-four hours a day. And I would like to say to the church, 'Wake up, and do what God wants you to do!'"

What a challenge the Hughes' story is to all of us comfortable and complacent baby boomers who feel like we've done our part and deserve a rest! These are people without lots of financial resources who have taken on a huge task and, by the grace of God, are giving ten children a new life and a fresh knowledge of Christ.

DOESN'T IT TAKE YEARS TO ADOPT A CHILD?

It doesn't necessarily take a long time to adopt a child, though under some circumstances it can be a very drawn-out process. But even a long wait is a small price to pay. If you've raised your children, and you've retired or are about to retire, and you worry about the world going to pot all round you, look at the Hughes' shining example of what a difference one couple can make for the kingdom of our Lord. When we get to the place where we don't have to go to work every day to make a living, we have tremendous opportunity to use that time to invest in the lives of others.

There's a big waiting list for babies to be adopted, but there's not a big waiting list for ten-year-olds and twelve-year-olds and fourteen-year-olds, particularly those that have problems and have had disadvantaged and deprived backgrounds. But each one is a person that God has a plan and a purpose for, that God has knitted and embroidered together in their mother's womb. And He wants them to fulfill the purpose that He created them for.

It may be that you are one of the instruments that can be used to really help them be what God created them to be. We've got to step in, as salt and light, and be the moms that these children don't have. To be the dads that these children don't have.

As my interview with Van and Shirley was winding down, the conversation turned again back to that mother who had ten kids by four different men, who abandoned them to steal food in order to live and gambled and drank away her welfare check. Van said, "You know what my goal is? To get that mother, if she sobers up, and get the kids and become friends and lead her to the Lord."

To that Shirley added, "I want people to know that changing a child's life in a positive way changes your life. It changes the community. It can change the whole United States. If every Christian family took in a child, and had them become a born-again believer, we would have a nation praying to Jesus."

Amen!

CHAPTER 12

WITH THE CROSS OF JESUS

CHRISTIANS ARE EMPOWERED TO TRIUMPH
OVER A FALLEN WORLD.

There are only three divinely ordained institutions in human society. Foremost among them is the home, the family ordained by God. The others are the church and the civil magistrate. Each of us has our responsibilities to each of those institutions. But first in importance above all is the home.

We have responsibilities in the home on several levels. First of all as children, we are called to honor our fathers and mothers. Then we have responsibilities as spouses, and later on we have specified duties as Christian parents. In the church we have responsibilities as parts of the members of the body of Christ to identify and develop our spiritual gifts and to be ministered to by the spiritual gifts of others. In that way, together we may plumb the depth and ascend the height and grasp the breadth of the love and power of our Lord Jesus Christ. Finally, we have a ministry to the world to be the salt and the light that God has called us to be.

WHY IS THERE SO MUCH FRICTION TODAY
BETWEEN GOVERNMENT AND THE CHURCH?

We all have responsibilities when it comes to the government.
We are obedient to the government for conscience's sake, ren-
dering unto Caesar the things that are Caesar's and unto God
the things that are God's. Romans 13 tells us that the civil
magistrate is ordained by God that we may live in peace as a
society: "Everyone must submit to the governing authorities,
for there is no authority except from God, and those that exist
are instituted by God. So then, the one who resists the authority is opposing God's command, and those who oppose it will
bring judgment on themselves. For rulers are not a terror to
good conduct, but to bad. Do you want to be unafraid of the
authority? Do good and you will have its approval. For government is God's servant to you for good" (vv. 1–4a).

The government also has obligations, and one of those is not
to interfere with the home and the church. One of our continuing difficulties in the second half of the twentieth century and
the beginning of the twenty-first is that too often the government has by default taken over functions that God intended
for the family. The problem is that when the demands of the
family, the church, and the state get all mixed up together,
being obedient to one means you have to disobey another.

For example, the Bible says we as parents have the responsibility for raising our children in the nurture and admonition
of the Lord. It doesn't say anything about the government raising children in the nurture and admonition of the Lord. The
primary responsibility is to be in the parents' hands, not the
government's. Now God doesn't hold us accountable for
knowing everything, but He does expect us to know more
about Him and His word today than we did yesterday. And He

expects us to know more about Him and His word tomorrow than we do today.

What's the greatest threat to Christianity in America?

In Jeremiah 6 beginning with verse 17, God describes his prophets as watchmen: "I appointed watchmen over you and said, 'Listen to the sound of the trumpet!' But you said, 'We will not listen.'" This was a metaphor that would have been extremely familiar to all the people who first read it.

Back then if you lived in a town of any size, it had a wall around it because about the only way you could protect yourself and secure your family and possessions was to build walls around everything. The walls were always manned by watchmen who would have their assigned watches on the walls so that no time day or night would there be a moment when there wouldn't be constant surveillance in every direction.

At the first sign that anything was amiss, these watchmen would blow their shofars—their ram's horn trumpets—to rouse the people from their beds if it was night, or to call them in from the fields and pastures if it was day. With this primitive security system in place, the townspeople could go about their business knowing the watchmen were there, and in fact could look up to see them at their posts on top of the wall.

Of course the passage I cited from Jeremiah speaks of a different kind of watchman—a spiritual watchman. The watchmen-prophets scanned the horizon and finally turned their gaze within the walls. What they saw happening inside the walls was of greatest concern to them. That's when they blew the warning blast to warn the people of impending spiritual disaster because the danger was inside, not outside the walls.

The situation of twenty-first-century America is very similar. We face a far greater peril from our own immorality and our own degradation and our own degeneracy than we ever faced from the Japanese navy or the German air force or the Soviet missile command.

Today's polling experts tell us more Americans than ever before are happy and confident about their economic present and future. In fact, more of them say they feel economically secure than at any time since the 1930s when data first started being collected. And yet at the same time, these same Americans have never been more pessimistic and more unhappy about their emotional present and future. The problem is that we've been trying to feed our spiritual need with material food and we're suffering from spiritual and emotional malnutrition. We have made idols of our material well-being and they have come back to haunt us.

There's a reason why what happened in the last fifty years in America isn't discussed as much as it should be. It's embarrassing to some of the people most likely to discuss it. There was too often a failure of faith and a failure of nerve in too many pulpits. Preachers insist that God is love. That's true. He loves you the way you are, but that doesn't mean He doesn't want you to change. Any answer that implies otherwise is a great lie perpetuated by the devil.

Too often we struggle with the popular image of God as some sort of cosmic Santa Claus—a jolly old fellow whom we can ask for what we want, and, if we've been good little boys and girls, He'll give it to us. The God of the Bible is nothing like that. He is our father, but He's also omnipotent and awesome and terrible in His power. God is our Father not our grandfather. Fathers spank; grandfathers spoil. It was a great revelation to me to watch my parents become grandparents. If they had raised me the way they dealt with their grandchildren, I'd be in the penitentiary.

WHAT'S THE MOST IMPORTANT CHALLENGE WE FACE IN SHAPING OUR FUTURE?

Whether or not America has a future worth having doesn't depend on what happens in Washington, D.C. It doesn't depend on the Supreme Court or Congress. It depends on parents and keepers of Christian households, and on many, many thousands of others like you who refuse to turn loose of their faith. "If my people, who are called by my name, will humble themselves and pray and seek my face . . . then will I . . . heal their land," says the Lord (2 Chron. 7:14).

Our government has separated itself from Judeo-Christian values and now there are rumblings about recombining them somehow. As encouraging as the idea is in the abstract, we must move ahead with caution. The last thing thinking Christians should ever want is for the government to sponsor and promote religion. Government should allow for the free exercise of people's faith, but that is a far different position than promoting religion. That would be like being squeezed by a python—all the life is wrung out of you and you fall over dead.

If you've ever been inside a magnificent European cathedral, along with the magnificent stonework and decoration, you may also have noticed that it was practically empty and spiritually dead. When the government sponsors religion, the government thinks it owns religion. The government thinks it can tell you how to express your faith, but it never gets it right, and it never will.

Roger Williams understood this in the seventeenth century. He said there needs to be a wall between the church and the state—*not* the kind of wall that the ACLU or Americans United for Separation of Church and State have perverted it to be, but a wall that keeps the wilderness of the world from coming in and corrupting the garden of the church. That's the problem: not that the church will corrupt the world, but the other way around.

SHOULD CHRISTIANS SUPPORT GOVERNMENT-SPONSORED "FAITH-BASED INITIATIVES"?

There's been a lot in the news about "faith-based initiatives," which is Washington doublespeak for church partnerships with government entities in order to deliver public services. I think the goals of the proposal are noble, and that the program as it's being developed can be a powerful tool for helping religion be more of a force for good in American society.

But when the government starts saying let's partner together and let's use some money to help you provide social services, watch out. Because with the king's shekels will ultimately come the king's shackles. They'll want a hand in how your church programs are administered and funded. And then you're in trouble.

If the government really wanted to empower faith-based groups, the swiftest and most effective method would be to allow all taxpayers to itemize their charitable contributions. By the government's own estimates, that would generate $14 billion, much of which would end up in church offering plates with no strings attached. This would be an effective use of the time-honored method of shaping tax policy to encourage people to spend money in ways that promote the general good of the country. (Tax breaks for home mortgages and retirement savings are successful examples of this process.)

How can we make America a more Christian nation?

If we want America to be a Christian nation there's only one way to do it—convert her citizens to faith in Christ. Help people get saved and understand that by being saved they should have a different value system, one based on biblical truth. Our ultimate allegiance as citizens is not to a political party. Our ultimate allegiance is to Jesus Christ alone, and we ought to vote our values, convictions, and beliefs as informed by Holy Scripture and let that take us where it will.

I deal with both Republicans and Democrats most days of the week and I can tell you both parties can use more help than all the Christians in the country can give them. Wouldn't it be wonderful if we could live to see the day when abortion is no longer a partisan issue? That's where we've come to on the race issue. Both parties are committed to racial reconciliation; the only difference of opinion is the best way to achieve it. But the most sinister and desperate attack in history on the American family, the legal murder of innocent babies in the womb, will haunt us until God's people get right with God and begin to be the salt and light He called us to be.

Change starts in our homes, extends to our churches, and moves on to every institution that affects our lives, twenty-four hours a day, seven days a week. It is our obligation and our responsibility to make the civil magistrate better reflect the values of the people, and to make sure people who rule over us are converted, or that at least they operate from a Christian perspective. As long as we believe the lie that we don't have the right to be involved in public policy, we will fall short of our goal, our obligation, and our responsibility.

WHAT EFFECT DO TWO-INCOME FAMILIES
HAVE ON SPREADING THE GOSPEL?

Dr. James Dobson rightly says the traditional family is "the most effective instrument ever designed to spread the Gospel of Jesus Christ. The vast majority of believers come to Christ when they are children, under the influence of their parents. If that institution breaks down, however, the faith of generations to come will be in jeopardy."

The family, according to Dobson, suffers from the seemingly universal tendency to live our lives faster and faster and try to do more and more every day. This trend "leaves every member of the family exhausted and harried. Many of them have nothing left to invest in their marriages or in the nurturing of children."

Fifty-nine percent of children come home to empty houses every afternoon "during which anything can happen," he notes, and this harried lifestyle puts the majority of its pressure on women torn between what they feel they should be and what their society demands of them. Many women "are trapped in a chaotic world that constantly threatens to overwhelm them."

Some of them "grew up in busy, dysfunctional, career-oriented households, and they want something better for their kids. And yet financial pressures and the expectations of others keeps them on a treadmill that renders them unable to cope."

Dobson boldly states what many Christian leaders have thought, I suspect, but have been too timid to admit publicly: "the two-career family *during the child rearing years* creates a level of stress that is tearing people apart. And it often deprives children of something they will search for the rest of their lives."

He predicts that if a "scale-back from this lifestyle, which I call 'routine panic,' ever grows into a movement, it will portend wonderfully for the family. It should result in fewer divorces and more domestic harmony. Children will regain the status they deserve and their welfare will be enhanced on a thousand fronts." The question is whether families will make the financial sacrifices necessary, or let the "nightmare of over-commitment" continue unchecked.

CAN'T SOCIAL AND SPIRITUAL DEVELOPMENT TAKE PLACE ON SEPARATE TRACKS?

The idea that there are two Gospels, a social Gospel and a spiritual Gospel, was hatched in the pits of hell. There is only one Gospel and it is a whole Gospel for whole people. It is a denial of the Gospel for Christians to seek to feed the hungry and not tell people about the bread of life. It is a denial of the Gospel to seek to house the homeless and not tell them that in our father's house are many mansions. It dishonors the incarnation of our Savior to talk about the bread of life and heaven and be insensitive to the fact that our hearers are hungry and homeless and thirsty.

Jesus has commanded Christians to be both salt and light. Salt is defensive in that it stops the decay and the degradation. Light is offensive: it dispels the darkness and illuminates the path. There are limitations to what the law can do. You can't legislate revival or reformation. However, if revival and reformation occur, they will be reflected in legislation and society's values.

The salt of the law can change actions, but it's only the light of the Gospel that can change attitudes. The salt of the law can change behaviors, but only the light of the Gospel can change beliefs. The salt of the law can change habits, but only the light of the Gospel can change hearts.

Here is the way it's supposed to work. We as Christians share our faith and, when people come to know Jesus as savior, their worldviews should change. When those with biblically informed worldviews reach critical mass, they then can begin to influence legislation. That's not called a theocracy, that's called the democratic process. It's the way slavery was eventually abolished. It's the way racial segregation was banished from the law. And it's the way Christians can restore once again to America a biblically based legal system that protects all human life from conception to natural death and everywhere in between.

What will restore America to its Christian roots?

We need a revival that ripens into an awakening and then becomes a reformation that shakes America for Jesus as Luther and Calvin shook Europe, as Whitefield and Wesley shook England, and as Edward and Whitefield shook colonial America for Jesus Christ. And that revival will begin at the firesides and dinner tables and on the porch swings of the American family.

Admiral Isoroku Yamamoto, descended from Samurai warriors, was the commander of the Japanese Combined Fleet and architect of the attack on Pearl Harbor. When the first reports came in of the stupendous success of the attack and the devastation of the American Pacific Fleet, there was a celebration aboard his flagship in Tokyo Bay. Then word came unexpectedly that through some bureaucratic miscommunication, including the fact that almost no one at the Japanese embassy in Washington on a Sunday could use an English language typewriter, the attack had come before diplomatic relations had been formally broken off.

Yamamoto canceled the celebration, went into seclusion in his stateroom and wrote these words in his diary: "I can think of nothing that will infuriate the Americans more. At Pearl Harbor we had hoped to strike a crippling and demoralizing blow. But I am fearful that all we have succeeded in doing is to awaken a sleeping giant and fill him with terrible resolve."

There are daunting challenges before us. But as Christian families, with the Bible as our guide, we are empowered to triumph over the temptations and assaults of a fallen world. The Bible, along with these examples of godly men and women who have prevailed by remaining true to biblical standards, gives Christians everything they need to defend their beliefs and to go on the offensive with confidence.

I believe that if you look out across the landscape of America today, seeking with the eye of faith and listening with the ear of hope, you will detect the rustlings of a long-slumbering giant called the people of God. Like the prodigal son, they awaken from their slumber and shake the filth from themselves and rise up determined to remember what it was like when man and culture and God were in accord. They realize the world is not that way anymore and resolve to repent and return and find restoration, to come home to the Father who faithfully and tirelessly scans the horizon waiting for that which was lost to come home. And they're determined that they're going to take their country with them.

May it begin here. May it begin now. May it begin with you.

RICHARD LAND

As president of the Southern Baptist Convention's Ethics & Religious Liberty Commission (ERLC), Richard Land champions the interests of the Christian faith and family. Equipped by God with a pastor's heart and a scholar's mind, Land stands in the gap on Capitol Hill and in the public square to plead for godliness and common decency. A graduate of Princeton (A.B., *magna cum laude*) and Oxford (D.Phil.) Universities, as well as New Orleans Baptist Theological Seminary (Th.M.), Dr. Land has served as a pastor as well as advisor to former Texas Governor William P. Clements Jr., Land thus possesses both the training and experience necessary to speak with authority on the ethical and public policy challenges facing families in America in the twenty-first century.

A nationally renowned authority in ethics, American and world history, religious liberty, and church-state issues, Land offers a fresh and insightful perspective that is highly sought after and widely respected. He has given testimony before committees in both Houses of the U.S. Congress. National media organizations including ABC, CBS, PBS, CNN, the *New York Times*, the *Wall Street Journal*, and *USA Today* interview Land when they need timely analysis on ethical, moral, cultural, political, governmental, and social issues. Land currently serves at the appointment of President George W. Bush as a member of the United States Commission on International Religious Freedom.

From its Washington, D.C.-based office tc its thirty-minute weekday radio program, *For Faith & Family*, heard weekly by 1.5 million listeners around the country, The Ethics & Religious Liberty Commission, directed by Land, works to keep the American public informed on critical issues facing the family and the nation.

JOHN PERRY

John Perry is a biographer, novelist, and freelance writer who received his B.A. *cum laude* from Vanderbilt University, with additional studies at University College, Oxford, England. He was a founding principal of American Network Radio, and has been an award-winning advertising copywriter and Gold Medallion finalist. His previous books include *Sgt. York: His Life, Legend and Legacy; The Vow: The Kim and Krickitt Carpenter Story;* and *Lady of Arlington: The Life of Mrs. Robert E. Lee.* He lives with his wife and two children in Nashville.

THE ETHICS & RELIGIOUS LIBERTY
COMMISSION (ERLC)

The ERLC, an agency of the Southern Baptist Convention (SBC) with offices in Nashville and Washington, D.C., is dedicated to addressing social and moral concerns and their implications on public policy issues from City Hall to the U.S. Congress. The SBC is the largest Protestant denomination in the nation with nearly 16 million members. Richard Land has served as president of the ERLC since 1988. Land and ERLC staffers are available to address your church or event on a wide range of ethical, moral, and social concerns.

Listed below are some of the ministries of the Ethics & Religious Liberty Commission.

Broadcast Division

Through *For Faith & Family*, a thirty-minute weekday radio program launched in 1998, Land speaks on the critical issues of the day to more than 1.5 million listeners each week on more than 550 stations across the country, with many more listeners tuning in each day on the Internet (www.faithandfamily.com).

Land's articulate and insightful discourse on the issues that are impacting families has generated a grassroots following that is inspired to preserve the distinctives that have made America great. Live and archived programs can be accessed via the Internet. *Insight*, a sixty-second commentary on the news, is delivered each day by Land as well.

Public Policy Division

Through its Washington, D.C., office, the ERLC secures a prominent evangelical presence on Capitol Hill and represents the interests and concerns of traditional families across the nation.

ERLC staff monitor key public policy issues and track and report on important developments in the legislative, executive, and judicial branches of the federal government. Staffers in this office endeavor to keep constituents throughout the nation apprised of the latest news of interest.

The D.C. office is known as Leland House, named for John Leland, a Baptist preacher whose persistent intercession with James Madison led to the U.S. Constitution's First Amendment, securing our freedom of religion and speech.

Research Division

Under Land's leadership, the ERLC's Research Institute brings together some of the brightest minds in the country to develop strategies for transforming the culture. Preserving the sanctity of human life and religious liberty, fostering racial reconciliation, fighting substance abuse, and eliminating the devastating effects of gambling, pornography, and world hunger are just a few of the efforts supported by this biblically grounded ministry.

The Research Division maintains an up-to-date library of over one thousand files on the moral, cultural, and religious liberty issues affecting families today. Its fact sheets, Bible studies, and sermon materials equip the pastor and the layperson with the knowledge and the tools to understand and change the culture and help families stay faithful to God.

Print & Interactive Division

The ERLC seeks to help families think biblically and act Christlike through *Light*, a full-color, bimonthly periodical, and *eSalt*, an electronic newsletter that focuses on public policy issues. The ministry also publishes *LifeLight*, a colorful and information-packed handout that focuses on a different ethical issue each month.

Articles in *Light* are crafted to help families integrate God's truths into their everyday life. The magazine examines critical issues that are troubling families and offers a biblical response. The magazine urges readers to engage the pressing cultural and social issues of our day with God's wisdom and strength as salt in a decaying culture and as his light in a sin-darkened society. Subscriptions to both publications are available for a contribution to the ministry.

The ERLC has an Internet presence at www.erlc.com. The site provides visitors valuable information on the moral and ethical issues of the day, as well as the means to keep abreast of developments in federal legislation and to contact elected representatives with a few simple keystrokes.

To receive a free product catalog or for more information on these and other services available through the ERLC, contact BY MAIL:

The Ethics & Religious Liberty Commission (SBC)
901 Commerce St., Suite 550
Nashville, Tennessee 37203

BY E-MAIL: www.erlc.com or
www.faithandfamily.com.

BY PHONE: 1–800–475–9127

NAME AND SUBJECT INDEX

SCRIPTURE INDEX